From Pills to

My Journey into Meditation

By

Midnight McBride

This Is Not A Book About Euthanasia!

Copyright © 2018 Midnight McBride

ISBN: 978-0-244-98461-8

All rights reserved, including the right to reproduce this book, or portions thereof in any form. No part of this text may be reproduced, transmitted, downloaded, decompiled, reverse engineered, or stored, in any form or introduced into any information storage and retrieval system, in any form or by any means, whether electronic or mechanical without the express written permission of the author.

Cover artwork by Midnight McBride.

All internal artwork by A. H. Smith

Main poetry by D. W. Parry

Photography by Martin Simpson
www.imagesbymartin.co.uk

'This manuscript presents inspiring and accessible material which offers the reader the chance to reflect on the nature of modern society, education, the media, spirituality, and the potential for meditation to ameliorate some of the effects of living in this high-stress, agenda-driven world. It cleverly blends tales from the author's own life, advice, ancient wisdom, and instruction with pockets of sparkling humour and curious tangents. The result is an exciting, well-paced book which gives the reader plenty to reflect on – perhaps in their next meditation session!'

Independent Professional Editor

FOREWORD

This book may seem like an uninterrupted stream of consciousness and awareness at first, but it has been intentionally written this way, just like a breathing meditation.

That is, having distracting thoughts, following them, and drifting away from the point of focus. Then recognising this and without becoming frustrated, accepting it, relaxing, and gradually bringing your attention back to that point. This is the oscillation and waveform of life, back and forth in a cyclical rhythm. Gently moving in one direction and then slowly returning. Accepting variations with no resistance. It's like the book is breathing and alive with a heartbeat.

Shalom

Midnight

Next - Book two

"MOVING FORWARD" - LEARNING HOW TO GLIDE

"When you think from a beautiful garden, you will see flowers everywhere!"—MM

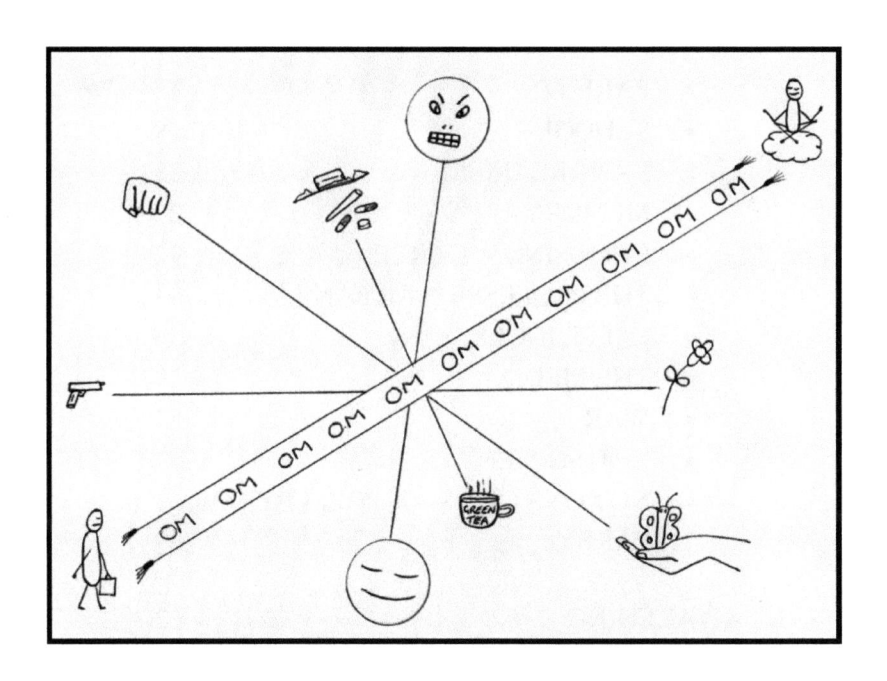

"MY JOURNEY INTO MEDITATION"

CONTENTS

1. INTRODUCTION — 1

2. CONDITIONING – "THE LIE" — 11

   - PARENTS — 12
   - SCHOOL — 18
   - DAYDREAMERS — 23
   - MEMORY — 27
   - CHOOSING A CAREER — 32
   - THE PROFESSIONAL FAN — 33
   - FALSE IDOLS — 44
   - THE MEDIA — 49
   - WAR — 55
   - YOUNG MEN — 57
   - NOT ONE OF US – A POEM BY D.W. PARRY — 69

3. AWAKENING — 72

   - MY STORY — 73
   - MY AWAKENING — 83
   - GOOD MENTAL HEALTH — 89
   - BEING HAPPY — 96
   - SANCTUARY OF THE MIND – A POEM BY D.W. PARRY — 100

4. MEDITATION 104
   - WHY DO WE NEED TO MEDITATE? 104
     - STRESS 106
     - A PRESENT MOMENT REACTION TO AN EXTERNAL EVENT 112
     - THOUGHTS ABOUT PAST AND FUTURE EVENTS 114
     - WORRY 124
   - WHAT IS MEDITATION? 130
   - MEDITATION JOURNEY – A POEM BY D.W. PARRY 131
   - WHAT ARE THE DIFFERENT TYPES OF MEDITATION? 134
   - DO I NEED TO BE A BUDDHIST TO MEDITATE? 141
     - MANJUSHRI AND RETREATS 142
     - THE ANSWER – A POEM BY MIDNIGHT MCBRIDE 151
     - BUDDHISM 158
   - WHAT ARE SOME OF THE DIFFERENT TECHNIQUES OF BUDDHIST MEDITATION AND HOW DOES IT WORK? 162
     - CONCENTRATION 165
     - VISUALISATION 172
     - OBSERVATION AND AWARENESS (MINDFULNESS) 176
       - MINDFUL OF ACTION 176
       - MINDFUL OF THOUGHT 178

- VOCALISATION (USING MANTRA) 180
  - OM MANI PADME HUM – A POEM BY D.W. PARRY 185
  - SOUND 188
- WHAT ARE THE PHYSICAL BENEFITS OF MEDITATION? 194
- WHAT ARE THE MENTAL BENEFITS OF MEDITATION? 198
- WHAT ARE THE SPIRITUAL BENEFITS OF MEDITATION? 206
- WHY IS EXERCISE ON THE LIST? 217
- IS MEDITATION THE ONLY WAY TO FIND INNER PEACE? 220
  - LONDON CONCERTANTE 221
  - NATURE 227
  - THE SEA AND GOING UNDERNEATH IT 231
  - SKYDIVING AND ADRENALINE 233

ACKNOWLEDGEMENTS 235

QUOTES 238

BIBLIOGRAPHY 253

ABOUT THE AUTHOR 259

1.INTRODUCTION

Hi, everyone.

My name is Midnight, also known as Patrick, also known as P.J.

I have written a short book to tell you about the profound effect that meditation has had on me. You could say it saved my life!

I currently travel around giving talks and teaching meditation as "Meditations by Midnight", but it wasn't always like this. My situation used to be very different.

My life has changed quite drastically over the last five years, since I first learned how to meditate and became a Buddhist, and I would like to share this journey with you. I have tried to break it down into the various stages I went through and the lessons I learnt along the way. Firstly, for those of you that knew me before I went through these changes, I would just like to apologise. You will have seen the mess I was in before, but also the incredible healing that has now taken place. My life is far from perfect, but it is several light-years away from where it used to be.

"To be better than you were yesterday is a great achievement. Do this every single day. This is the path to enlightenment."— MM

Lots of people may know part of me, but only a few know the whole truth. You see, I wasn't completely honest with myself or others about who I really was. I compartmentalised my life, so very few people got the full picture. I didn't even know I was doing it. This is a common tactic employed by governments and politicians.

"You can't build the truth on a lie." —MM

You see, we are like a sculpture, a fine work of art. Chip, chip, chip. Taking small steps. Slowly shaping our lives with every thought. We are our own Michelangelo. All we ever have is this moment. The challenges we meet and the choices we make, right now. Yesterday is gone. Tomorrow is not here yet, and when it does come, it will be this moment. So the rest of your life will be based on the next decision you make. No pressure here then. Everything from this point forward is built on this moment and then it will become this moment. So, you see, everything is "now". Starting right now, by making one good decision, and then another, you have just changed your life, the world, and the universe that surrounds it. You are the sculptor and the sculpture.

I have been and done many things in my life. Some of them are probably best left out of this book to prevent unnecessary hurt!

"You can start in the sewers and finish in the stars!" —MM

Here are just a few of the gentler topics, to illustrate a point:

"I" have spent twenty years managing tunnelling projects.

"I" have been skydiving.

"I" have been scuba diving.

"I" have been a fighter (MMA and on the street).

"I" have been an actor (supporting).

"I" have taken lots of drugs and I have drunk lots of alcohol.

"I", "I", "I", etc.

Through searching for happiness, I have tried a whole variety of activities and discovered three things:

1. **Although they temporarily provided pleasure, none of these things made me happy.**
   You see, pleasure is experienced in the material world and it is fleeting and transient at best. It will only ever provide short-term relief from our problems. Joy, on the other hand, comes from within. This is our natural state, and once we learn to get out of the way and quieten our minds and become still through meditation, it will evolve naturally. If you're looking for happiness in the outside world, in the realm of the five senses, you are looking in all the wrong places. You will never find it there. You have to look inside. The doors open inwards.
   "You can go within, or go without." — MM (Paraphrased from Ralph Waldo Emerson)

2. **It's not all about me ("I").**
   Your primary purpose while in this spacesuit we call a body is to be happy, but also to help others. To spread joy, peace, and love to everyone that you meet.

3. **You must follow your heart (follow your dharma).**
   When you are on the right path you will feel inspired, experience bliss and synchronicity, have boundless energy, and be moving in harmony with Natural Law. This is the path of least resistance.

This book is a journey. From pills to peace. From the darkness into the light.

Please don't be put off by Chapter One (Conditioning – "The Lie").

It's not all doom and gloom, but we have to take an honest look at ourselves and the state of affairs in the world in order to address the issues and move forward.

You have to recognise and acknowledge a problem before you can start to resolve it.

After "The Lie", the book and my journey change course, going from strength to strength, and moving in a positive direction towards inner peace and bliss.

In order to cultivate new flowers, first we must weed the garden. Empty your cup, if you will, and make space for new content.

This takes great strength, but the other option is to stay asleep.

Buddha is a Sanskrit word and literally means "the awakened one".

"It takes great courage to step into the light."—MM

"The more light you emit, the more darkness is revealed!"—MM

"When you emit your inner light, you can see other people in the dark."—MM

You have to move into the darkness and then shine.
The brighter your flame, the more darkness you will see, but as soon as you shine your light upon it, it becomes light too! Darkness cannot exist in the light.
Literally lighting up the world around you—this is the path to enlightenment. Then you realise that love and light is all there is. So in order to fix anything, we have to face it head on.
I know it's easier to just eat McDonalds and watch television but, people, you know this is not the truth. There is so much more to life. However, to see change, you have to first make changes.

"If you follow the herd, you won't be heard!"—MM

"SHEEP"

"Be the change that you wish to see in the world." — M. Gandhi

Stage one is the hardest. Acceptance. This means acknowledging the truth.
Like swallowing the "red pill" in the film *The Matrix*.
Warning! In doing this, you are driving down a one-way street. As much as you might try, you can't unknow something. You can't be put back into the box.
You have already started to evolve and grow, just by accepting what is. Looking with your eyes wide open. Once you have read this book you will view the world very differently. You will see it honestly and as it actually is. I am here to challenge your existing thought patterns, and it won't be an easy ride. It can be quite uncomfortable at first, but beautiful green pastures await once you get over the hill.

Once you know there is a problem, you have two choices.
You can either continue to numb the pain with drugs, cigarettes, and alcohol to get through the day, and then go and buy some more stuff that you don't really need to distract yourself from truth. Or you can act.

"You don't have to see the whole staircase. Just take the first step."—Martin Luther King Jr.

"All of humanity's problems stem from man's inability to sit quietly in a room alone."—Blaise Pascal

There is nowhere to hide in the silence.

We have to start being completely honest with ourselves. Only then can we make real change.

As you will see, in this book I use many different terms from different sources. I try to use the ones that are most easily understood.

I was brought up a Catholic but I have been a practicing Buddhist for the last five years now and I also practice transcendental meditation. Confused yet?

I have read many Buddhist texts, but have also read a lot of Dr Wayne Dyer, Eckhart Tolle, Deepak Chopra, and others.

Hence, indirectly, I have also read Carl Jung, Abraham Maslow, and many other great minds who some of these authors refer to.

I just try to use the simplest and most relevant term in any particular instance. I don't wrestle with it too much however; otherwise I would never finish this book.

I usually use the one that makes the most sense to me, avoiding some of the more complicated or less well-known Buddhist terms.

Here are some examples of more obscure terms:

The Buddhist term for the false self or ego is "self-grasping ignorance".

The Buddhist term for the subtle energies in the body is the "inner winds".

The Buddhist term for matters of the heart is the "mind".

Confusing, isn't it?

The Buddhist term "meditation" may also be referred to as "stillness" or "going into the gap".

The Buddhist term "inner peace" may also be referred to as "pure consciousness" by the practitioners of transcendental meditation, for instance.

I use the term "God" frequently also, but by this I mean the unified field or intelligent system that surrounds everything and connects us all.

You get the idea. There is no point in using terms that are not generally understood. If I feel it is imperative, I may use a less well known term, but in that instance, I will give a full explanation. I will not use, for example, "Mahamudra" or "Lamrim number twenty-one: Emptiness". They are much harder to grasp and explain properly. It would take a whole book, and besides, that's not why I'm here. My purpose is not to try and help a few people become enlightened, nor is it to preach Buddhism. For the record, I don't teach Buddhism, although I am obviously heavily influenced by it; I teach meditation and correct thought. My purpose is to help as many people as possible master the basic techniques of meditation, to reduce stress and then develop inner peace.

"Meditation is for everyone!"—MM

Anyway, that's enough of that. I am just going to use the best terms I can.

Through my experiences from giving talks, meditation sessions, and workshops, I have learnt that people love to use the most extreme or obscure examples to try and test a general principle, theory, or system of logic, so I may use a few of these in this book, both to test the principles in question and also for my own personal comedic entertainment.

"To be told something once is to be informed. To be told something again and again is to be conditioned. You are now being programmed." —MM

"Rather a wild flower than a potted plant." —MM

"CONDITIONING"

2. CONDITIONING – "THE LIE"

Question everything!

Please understand that I love you, Mum and Dad.

These are general principles—so don't take this personally.

It's not about you.

If you want a light read, turn around now—please proceed straight to Chapter Four— Meditation (but then you won't know why we need to do it!)

PARENTS

So let's rewind, right back to the beginning, to birth. We are born into this world uncorrupted, perfect beings in every way, still connected to the spirit realm. We are still in direct contact with the unified field. Our big toe is permanently dipped in pure consciousness without even trying. We have the energy of the universe flowing through us at 100 mph. We have a bat phone with a direct line straight to God. After all, we are all connected and made from the same stuff, star dust from the Big Bang, and are therefore all still quantumly entangled. We all have God and therefore seeds of divinity within us. It's just that we become increasingly detached from this as we get older. We can reconnect at any time, or even stay connected all the while with the application and practice of correct principles and thought. However, on the whole, we lose our way. With a newborn child, and usually for the first few years of its life, the door to the spirit realm is still wide open. At this point we are still tethered to the creator, the intelligent system, and have unlimited potential. We only know how to be ourselves and we are egoless. Babies don't lie. This is bad programming and is a skill they have to learn from us. They are completely honest. They smile when they are happy and cry when they are in discomfort. I believe that they, just like dogs, can hear things we cannot. Babies can also see things we cannot. I have been in a very old listed building which is now a restaurant and seen a young child in a high chair staring at one spot for the entire meal. This spot appeared to be just fresh air and empty space to everyone else. I wasn't the only person to notice and see this spectacle. The child was laughing and interacting with this space, as if there were someone in front of them. Then, later on, I found out some of the history of that place and what had happened there hundreds of years earlier. This building was apparently still visited by another child. Haunted, if you like. Yes, I believe babies can see outside the electromagnetic spectrum and into the non-physical spirit realm.

Anyway, I have a terrible habit of drifting, getting off point and then going off on tangents. I like tangents. I just love following something and seeing where it leads. Sometimes I surprise myself.

I use the term "God" a lot, as explained earlier, but I don't mean an old man with a white beard and a big ego, a god who gets upset, angry, and jealous, or a god who judges everyone and punishes people for their sins. Oh no. I mean God as in the universal force that flows through us all and is everywhere. The intelligent system that we are connected to and that is within everyone.

So at this young age we are pure, inspired in every moment, and constantly daydreaming. We are full of great ideas and all we can do is think of all the things that can go right. We don't, like adults, automatically start to make a list of all the reasons not to do something, all the things that could go wrong, and talk ourselves out of doing anything by overthinking it and living in fear. As young bringers of light, we are hardwired to succeed. All we do is have an idea, believe that we can achieve it, and do it. We know we can. Doubt hasn't been invented yet. All our decisions are based on what will make us happy. The answers to all the questions posed and challenges we face come from within and are derived out of love and passion, not fear. Later on in life, most of our decisions are made from the bad programming that we have then been given.

For example:

Should I be an artist or a banker?

Well, which will make me the most money?

There is only one way to truly succeed and that is to follow our dharma. This is our purpose; what makes us happy, what fills us up with joy, what inspires us, and hence puts us in a state of bliss. When we are fulfilling our dharma we become fully present. This is when we immerse ourselves in the realm of the five senses, in the now, when time stands still and we get lost in the moment. Just being!

"I am a human being, not a human doing."—Dr Wayne Dyer

When we follow our dharma, we are swimming downstream, in the same direction as and being carried by the flow of universal energy, and this inevitably also benefits all of mankind.

Hold on a second. I will need to back up a bit again! So, we are born into this world as pure beings and then we interact with it. Our environment influences us and this is also where we get our first batch of data. All being well, we will initially interact with our parents. Now, before we began our journey and popped out into this realm, our parents and their parents before them had been programmed by the system and their parents too. So with some new modifications of their own thrown in to boot, off our parents went. They began to programme us.

As humans, we are an accumulation of everything that has ever happened to us. A product of our environment and our experiences. This doesn't mean we are defined by our past. Quite the contrary. This is just how we learn. Initially, we have no option but to take the information provided.

We are like a sponge for information, like little Vileda super mops, and can pick up behaviours, lessons, and data faster than they can be dished out.

If, like me, it can take forty years before you start to figure out that some of the information given wasn't necessarily correct or right for you, and then you can start to re-programme.

However, in most cases (and I know some people had a very tough childhood), on the whole, parents simply do their best from the programming and memes that were given to them and they usually do it with love. There are no rulebooks.

A "Meme" is a term from a book called *"Virus of the Mind"* by Richard Brodie.

An example of a meme would be "Better safe than sorry" or "You can't teach an old dog new tricks". These are old thought patterns that have been passed down through the generations. Don't get me wrong, they aren't all bad. There are some corkers too. "There are no pockets in a shroud" is very profound, and these are very wise words indeed.

I suppose all we can ever really do is to refine the data given to us, taking the best bits from our parents and becoming a slightly better version of humanity in each generation, and, in theory, in about 200 years we will all be enlightened!

If you think this seems like a slightly harsh or stern view, think about corporal punishment, apartheid, and sexism. All commonplace, just one generation ago.

Like I said, there is a lot of good stuff too. Some of the programming given to us is wonderful and we can try to emulate and perpetuate this. We need this contrast though to know the good from the not-so-good. However, it is the bad programming we need to identify and focus on initially, to take a look at what we are dealing with and then how to tackle the job in hand. It is only by knowing the darkness, but not dwelling in it or on it, that we can then start to move towards and become the light. We need to navigate.

I watched a programme about two young children from Greenland. They lived in a yurt with their parents and had been home-schooled. They had never seen a television or watched the news, for example. They had never drunk a can of Coke or eaten any processed food or refined sugar. They had never really experienced feelings of jealousy, stress, bullying, or anger. Although they were six and eight years old at the time, they still possessed the childlike wonderment we were all born with, seeing magic all around them and in everything they encountered. This is before we start to label, compartmentalise, and judge as we get older.

"Once you label me, you negate me."—Dr Wayne Dyer

They had never worn a pair of Nike trainers or used a mobile phone. They were literally pure beings of light, little stars shining positive energy out into the universe, unaffected by the material world we all live in. They had not yet caught the disease and madness that infects the rest of humanity, the insanity which we call greed. They were fully present and alive in every sense of the word. Now I am not saying we all have to go and live in yurts, but what I am saying is that we don't realise how much we are conditioned by our environment. These two children were untouched by the modern society that we call progress. They were in perfect health, living in bliss and surrounded by nature. Tell me how the Western world can add to that?

We could learn a lot from some of the indigenous people of the world, who are still very much connected to the land and Mother Earth. They realise that you never really own anything and some of them can clearly see that the westernised civilisations of the world, are on the whole, quite mad. They know that collectively we have a disease of the mind, infected with bad thought patterns like stress, anger and greed.

So up to this point we have been programmed by our parents, but then this is where the system kicks in and really takes hold—we go to school!

SCHOOL

The best way to teach anyone anything is by example. Be the light!

To learn anything fully, to know it, you must experience it.

For example, I can describe a view to you and I can sketch it for you, but unless you see it with your own eyes, you can't know it. The best thing I can do is enjoy the view, then be the light and live in bliss; you will see the joy in my eyes and want to know why I am so happy. "It's the view," I say. I can then tell you where it is and invite you to come along with me and see it for yourself.

"Each time you raise yourself up, invite everyone to come and see the view."—MM

Also, just a point I want to make here, folks, before we start - boarding school. What the hell?

Try to imagine this from a child's eyes. The only two people in the world that absolutely, 100% have your best interests at heart, in theory, are your parents. They brought you into this world and are supposed to love you unconditionally, and then they send you away.

That child must be highly inconvenient!

These schools are often a breeding ground for success. That is, success defined in the material world sense: obtaining wealth, possessions, status, and power. If you are a success in this system and you fit in then you have actually failed. This is not your nature or your true self. You bought "The Lie". Politicians and people in other high-end jobs are often bred here and that's how these schools are sold. Unfortunately, if you find someone hanging from a door by his necktie with an orange in his mouth attempting auto-erotic asphyxiation, he usually went to a boarding school and got buggered by his master or the head of his dorm and thus started down the road of self-harm and, if not, at the very least, S&M. They are also a breeding ground for perversion. I know you may think this is a sweeping generalisation and a very dark or bleak point of view, but it's correct. When was the last time you heard of a forklift truck driver or a milkman attempting auto-erotic asphyxiation? I will guess never.

Remember, it's time to start being honest here folks. Enough nonsense.

So, for the people out there that went to boarding school, were glad to see the back of their parents, and are now well-balanced human beings and not emotionally scarred for life, I am very grateful you made it through the system.

"Well, it didn't do me any harm!"

However, for those of you who have or are about to put your kids into that system or even back into the exact same boarding school you went to, please think twice and reconsider.

If I said that a large number of Catholic priests are paedophiles and that this truth was hidden for many years, and that the priests were protected by the church and this fact was also ignored by the police, would I be lying? Is this a sweeping generalisation? Am I being over the top? Watch the film *Spotlight*. It's a true story.

Remember, "It takes great courage to step into the light."— MM

This team of reporters met a lot of resistance and still did the right thing, regardless of the risks, the threats they received, and the consequences to themselves.

The majority of priests in Boston were in on it. That's right, the majority. That means more than half. However, because no one had the full picture or perspective, it went on for years. If they weren't actually committing the acts, they were complicit. The abuse was compartmentalised and all the cases were made to look like isolated incidents. To anyone that was not actually involved in the cover-up, it was impossible to see the extent or full scale of the problem.

To date, over $85 million has been paid out to 552 victims. This is just to the ones that survived and had a voice. Multiple suicides occurred here because of this failing system.

Anyway, I will leave this topic now. I have vented.

It's all just a dream anyway. I remind myself of this frequently. This alleviates a lot of stress for me. Bill Hicks had it down: "It's just a ride."

Right, so, you arrive for your first day at school.

Initially, they start by getting you into a structured daily routine. To conform.

Getting you used to sitting in a box (a classroom), doing and learning things that you don't want to, for hours on end each day, and definitely not doing what makes you happy. Training you to do as you're told and not to follow your dharma, dreams, and inspirations. Yes, basically preparing you for adulthood. I am still staggered by the number of people who voluntarily go and sit in a box or cubicle for eight hours a day plus, staring at a computer screen, doing something that makes them miserable, in a room that quite often has no natural light or fresh air. Firstly, this is the definition of control and insanity, and secondly, we do have a choice! This is just bad programming again, folks. Most of us feel like victims with no options left, stuck in the system.

"We have to do this to pay the bills."

Pay different bills. Don't pay the bills. We don't need all the stuff we have anyway; sell it. Go bankrupt and start again. You will survive. How badly do you want change? Are you prepared to waste even one more day?

However, you're not alone in this endeavour. If this is you? Well, I have done this too, for most of my life. Nearly every mistake that can be made, I have made it. That is how I learned to navigate and to change.

We are human beings. We are meant to roam free and commune with nature, breathing in fresh air and bathing in sun light. Having new experiences every day.

It's amazing that through bad programming we can imprison ourselves, doomed to a life of misery.

"The prisons we all live in are constructed by the mind." —MM

DAYDREAMERS

"The fools who dream." —*La La Land*

I love music but I'm not a huge fan of musicals. However, if you get the chance, listen to the lyrics of the song *The Fools Who Dream,* from the film *La La Land.* It is all about daydreamers, the people who follow their hearts and live their dharma. Truly beautiful.

It is the daydreamers that usually have the most creative minds. They compose musical masterpieces, write books of poetry, paint great works of art, design rockets and space stations, and are also responsible for most of the incredible inventions in today's society.

However, if you're a daydreamer in school, you don't fare well. You keep wandering off into thought, drifting away from the material world that surrounds us and for this reason you get into trouble. They say, "He is a daydreamer," as though it were a bad thing. Each time you go off into another place, into a realm of fantasy. You are still connected. You're regularly inspired and the right side of your brain is still functioning correctly, in harmony with the left. Once you are fully tied down into this physical plane, the right side of the brain, which is responsible for your emotions, creativity, and intuition, is suppressed and almost completely shut down. The left side then takes over due to bad programming and sensory overload. We usually spend the next forty years trying to switch it back on again and restore the balance. Then, all being well, once we get there, we will go through the shift and spiritually awaken. See, once you realise you are disconnected from source energy and get a glimpse of your true nature, there is only one thing you want to do. This is to reconnect with the divine and open up the door once again.

"The doors open inwards, and inside, there are no sides."—MM

I was fortunate enough to experiment with the world of floatation tanks many years ago, when they first became available to the public. I won't give you a full description here, but the purpose was to experience total sensory deprivation (TSD), in order to switch off the left side of the brain and induce a sort of CPR to the right. What a ride! A story for my next book maybe.

Two other things that I now know can recreate and restore this balance are certain pieces of classical music and meditation. This has been proven scientifically.

There is, however, a surefire way to break this pattern and stop the right side of the brain from shutting down in the first place.

That is quite simply to be yourself and follow your bliss.

"Once understood, freedom is an unstoppable force, because it is born of the mind."—MM

So we are programmed by the schooling system.

We are told that winning is everything, that we must compete to succeed, and that your wealth is quantifiable by the amount of money you have. We are told that success is made up of possessions, power, and status, and that this in turn will lead to happiness. That our worthiness and position in society will be determined and judged by how much stuff we have. The more possessions we own, the better people we are. This is very bad programming and, of course, all nonsense.

We are fed total rubbish and this will lead to a life of misery.

In fact, going along with this theory, all the rich people in the world are happy and all the poor people in the world are miserable, right? Wrong!

"The more you have, the less you see." —MM

So because of our conditioning, in general, every decision we make is based on what will make us the most money. They have invested years of programming in us and consequently, as human beings, we are getting it all wrong! We are way off the mark.

They force us to conform and try to turn us into machines.

Ironically, the most important lesson you could learn at school is good mental health. This is made up of correct thinking, stress relief, stress management, and good communication skills. I like to call this "Happy Class". It's the most important job they have, and it's not even on the syllabus. I can't believe they don't teach the one thing we all need to learn!

There is no "Happy Class". What's going on?

This would definitely involve meditation, of course.

"If every eight-year-old in the world is taught meditation, we will eliminate violence from the world within one generation."
— Dalai Lama

This is very true, but I have something to add. Even in the future, with meditation being a common place practice for all of the children across the planet, if we, the adults, don't start to think correctly, we will still override their pure light with the bad programming that we give to them. Remember, their minds are like sponges for knowledge and we feed them the information. So to be clear, for this to work, everyone has to be involved. For all the children in the world to learn how to develop inner peace, we would have to teach them how to meditate but also show them how to think correctly. We can't do this until we practice it ourselves first. So it's not up to them, it's up to us! Be the light!

MEMORY

Just a quick note. I have the ability to remember the lyrics and a great amount of detail about the music from my childhood. This was when I was almost permanently in the now, fully present and in a state of bliss. Music can be very powerful and can trigger many emotions. It can resonate with and trigger your feelings. So Kool & the Gang and Earth, Wind and Fire are embedded upon my brain, and I don't just mean one or two of their songs. I can remember the tunes and recite all the words to thousands of songs effortlessly. Does this tell you something? Has the penny dropped yet?

When we are happy and in a state of joy, we can learn much more efficiently. Far more effectively than when we are unhappy. In fact, when we are stressed or in discomfort, nothing usually goes in at all. When a child is in trouble at school and struggling in class, if you can put a smile back on their face, they start to learn again. "Happy Class!"

I was taught that God gets angry, that he judges people because of their sexuality, and that he doesn't value women as much as men. I could go on. These are all the traits of men, not God, and so they are all lies too.

At no point in my educational career did anyone ever ask me what made me happy. What inspired me? What did I enjoy?

To enjoy is to be in-joy. Joy from within! That's where you will find it, inside yourself.Nobody told me to follow my intuition and do what makes my heart sing.

I use this analogy sometimes: we are like a computer. This is the terminology I use. I am going back a few years now, but when I was at school, they had just two types of memory:

Read Only Memory (ROM—this cannot usually be changed) — like the formative years of childhood.

Random Access Memory (RAM — this can be re-programmed) — like adulthood.

I will use an example from my life to illustrate this.

I got mugged in Manchester when I was thirteen by three much older lads. They beat the hell out of me. I was in shock afterwards. I was with two other boys, but they were young too. They just watched and cried because they were frightened and to be honest, they couldn't have done much about it anyway. I refused to give the bullies my new Adidas Colorado tracksuit top. I can laugh about it now but it wasn't very funny then. It was the first proper good hiding I got. They split my lip open and bust my face up pretty good. I was covered in blood.

My point is, it took me a long time to get over this episode and it probably scarred me emotionally.

I estimate that in my teens, twenties, and yes, even into my late thirties, sadly, I had well over a hundred fights on the streets of Bolton. The actual figure is probably much higher than this but I stopped counting. In my twenties and other low periods of my life, it was a weekly occurrence. Although admittedly I often started the fight and usually did most of the punching, causing a lot more hurt to others than they did to me. These are not the proudest moments of my life, but they are still part of my journey to arriving in this moment. My point is that I got over these episodes far more quickly, like water off a duck's back. If I got hurt, it wasn't a problem. My mind had become used to dealing with this process.

You see, ROM is very much like the programming and memories from the formative years of our childhood. These memories and experiences are used to programme our subconscious mind. A lot of this programming is very important, very hard to change, and deep down affects every decision we make. It is crucial to the construct of the person that we have become today. The things that happen to us and the programming at this young age usually affect us for the rest of our lives. If something traumatic happens, we can be mentally scarred from it. We may have to rebuild the computer in order to fix it!

Then adulthood comes along and the system switches over to RAM. This programming is all the new memories and experiences that we have from this point forward and it can be changed far more easily. Even bad experiences can be re-programmed with much less effort. However, this still requires a conscious decision to change from the person involved. They have to want to get better and heal. In some cases to remove the unwanted programming, the system needs to be switched off completely and rebooted, in others just reset daily, just like a real computer.

There are several ways to achieve this switch off, which is sometimes called the death of the ego, the shift, or a spiritual awakening. For example, this can be done voluntarily, such as with plant medicine, or involuntarily, such as through illness. There are many other ways this can happen or to do this. To gradually reset the system and facilitate this process yourself, a regular daily meditation practice can be used.

So after we finish our education, we leave school and probably for the first time start to think for ourselves. We then realise that the teachers and our parents who taught us are not gods, and are in fact just human beings like the rest of us and therefore also make mistakes. However, this breakthrough comes after our ROM has already been programmed.

As I joked earlier, I use sweeping generalisations a lot and, as always, there are exceptions to every rule. Life is full of contradictions and dichotomies. We are human, after all.

I think most teachers start out with the correct motivation and good intentions. They believe that they are going to change the world by educating the children within the current schooling system and are often, in my experience, lovely people.

The system is designed to gradually suck the life out of them too, with lots of red tape and also by not providing them with the tools, resources and freedom they need to make real progress. After time passes, in most cases, they eventually give up the fight. They then start to toe the line and become engrained into the very system they wanted to change.

"In order to fly, you must first learn how to spread your wings." —MM

"CHOOSING A CAREER"

CHOOSING A CAREER

Children are the most perfect expression and creations of God and have the divine light within them. The system is designed to programme them to do as they are told, to conform, to live in fear, and to always make decisions based on monetary gain and what other people think of them. Assuming they are lucky enough to make it to college, most of them are in serious debt and highly stressed before they even get a job and start work. The decks are stacked against them and they haven't even got off the runway yet.

So let's say you're about to decide upon a career path, because at fifteen years of age you definitely know what that will be, right? You know what you want to do for the rest of your life, right? Wrong! I still don't know what I want to be when I grow up! This may be one of the most important decisions you'll ever make, but don't panic; it's a lot easier than you think.

Do what makes you happy!

Any decision based purely on financial gain is a bad one. You should be asking yourself, does this make me happy? Does it benefit the people around me?

THE PROFESSIONAL FAN

A. So, you chose a career and you take the option based on what will make you the most money. Most of us do this. In this one fell swoop, you are doomed to a life of misery. You see, you may earn a good wage, but you are not following your heart or your dharma, which is your life's purpose. So each day you turn up to work for ten or maybe twelve hours, doing something you don't want to. This becomes a mechanical joyless endeavour. You don't feel any inspiration, which comes from the spirit within, in-spirit. You don't feel enthusiastic, which means to be divinely inspired. You get paid well, but you're miserable. When you finish work you are too tired to do the things you love because you don't sleep well. You don't sleep well because your mind is so busy. So to relieve the stress, turn off your mind, and get some sleep, you use chemicals. Not necessarily illegal ones at first either. Some legal drugs by the way are far worse for you than any illegal substances. I mean, just think of the mistake God made when he invented cannabis, an illegal drug but at the same time a plant with huge medicinal benefits. For what it's worth, in my opinion, if you take drugs you are not a criminal. You might need professional help or you may in some cases just be having fun, but you are definitely not a criminal. Anyway, I digress. So you smoke, drink, and maybe do a bit of cocaine at the weekends to switch off, but you're still miserable. It is okay though, because you earn a good wage, right? You will never be the best at what you do because when you finish work, you just want to get out of there. You did unpaid overtime for ten years and didn't get that damn promotion anyway. Your career ladder is capped because you hate your job. You inadvertently capped it yourself. We all basically sell our time and energy, the most precious commodities and gifts we have, to the highest bidder. I have done some hideous jobs for money in my time. Spending up to twenty hours a day, most of it underground, working seven days a week, for months on end. Basically it was hell on earth for me. Humans generally don't utilise all the best things in life that are free. Walking, swimming, running, and of course being in nature are all at our disposal. It is only when we are deprived of them, that we realise they are taken for granted. When you spend twenty hours a day in a hole, you gain perspective. Anyway, so you start spending that wage trying to distract yourself from your unhappy existence and buy new stuff that you don't need, but you look cool, right? You also get a bigger house and a faster car. Great, now you're in debt too. You feel trapped. Now you've figured out that all of that stuff doesn't make you happy for more than five minutes, and you realise that it's actually your life choices that were wrong, you want to change your job, but you can't. If you switch career in your forties, you will have to take a huge cut in wages and this won't pay your bills, loans, credit cards, mortgage, and secret drug habit. What about the wife and kids? They have become accustomed to a certain standard of lifestyle and take at least two holidays a year. If I don't get the kids what they want for Christmas, that's just cruel, isn't it? You're doomed and stuck, trapped in the system. The only joy you have left is watching your kids grow up happy, right? Going back into the exact same system that has killed your spirit, stolen your freedom and caused you to

become depressed. You feel like you are slowly dying inside. I mean, what's the point anymore? They would be better off without me, right? Maybe I should just leave this place. I don't feel well. I'm so stressed!
Maybe it's all that poisonous processed food and pop that I have been putting into my body for years. Maybe it's because I don't exercise anymore, because I have no energy, because I'm depressed? I have just been diagnosed with cancer. There's nothing I can do.
Wrong, wrong, wrong, wrong, wrong! You are a child of the universe. You are an infinite being. You have unlimited potential and are made of stars. You can do anything. You just need to pause and breathe. You need to do some personal work and start looking inside yourself for the answers. It's never too late. It's time to reconnect. It's time to go within. It's time to meditate, my friend!
There is, however, a better path, one without reaching breaking point before you awaken.
Now, let's rewind.
Option B.

"No matter what, someone always has to go first!"—MM

B. So you decide to choose a career option based on what will bring you the most joy instead.
If you love what you do, you will never work another day in your life.
You decide you're going to be a professional fan.
A what? A professional fan. That's right folks, a person who watches other people doing sports and supports

them. But there is no such thing! I know. I will be the first. A pioneer.

But how will you make a living? I haven't got a clue! I just know it will work out! I have faith. I am F.A.I.T.H.

I am a drag queen at the weekends. Only kidding, but an important point to note here. You don't have faith you become it. I will cover this in more detail later on.

So off you trot with absolutely no idea what you're doing or how you're going to do it.

"If you want to sail far, you have to sail close to the wind."—MM

What you do know is that as a child growing up, all your fondest memories were of going to watch things with your dad. Local sports events, competitions, and shows. You see, you remember the look of joy in the eyes of someone you cheered for, especially when they had no idea who you were. So, having no idea and absolutely no clue about what's next, you're just simply going to do what you love. This is what Deepak Chopra calls "the wisdom of uncertainty"!

"If you don't jump, you can't fly."—MM

You see, when you do what you love, you feel alive. You're full of beans and very enthusiastic about what you're doing, and this shows. People can see how happy you are and it makes them feel good too. It's not really like work at all, and because you love what you do, you become very good at it, putting all your boundless energy into the activity. So you decide to dress up as a big yellow bird and to make banners for the underdogs of every event you go to. The next one is a baseball game. You know it's the lead pitcher's birthday on that day. So you put that on a banner, still having no idea how you're going to pay your bills, but knowing one thing for sure, that you are following your dharma. You are then in alignment with the present moment and always living in the now.

"The universe will correspond to the nature of your song."—Reverend Michael Beckwith

You will then start to experience what Carl Jung calls "synchronicity". This is where the universe starts to conspire to help you. Everything just starts to fall into place.
During the game, the pitcher sees the banner you made and runs over to give you a big hug. Some of the local press were at the stadium covering the game. The evening paper and local TV station both run with the story: "Big Bird Gets Big Hug". Then the next day, you get a phone call.

"Hello, my friend. I know this might seem like a strange request, but will you come and watch my son's soccer game as Big Bird? It's his birthday too. We saw you on the

TV and it's all he talks about. It made him cry. Happy tears though, you understand. Could you make a banner? We will pay you."

"Well, of course. I would love to do that. It would be my pleasure."

So now you are getting paid to do what you love. See, when you love what you do, you will be very good at it, being inspired with new ideas all the time. You will be a real success without ever trying to make money; it will just come to you. The energy of the universe is flowing through you at 100 mph. The TV Company ring you asking if they could do a follow up story and a have a quick chat on camera. "Who is Big Bird?"
They air the interview clip on the early morning show. By lunchtime, your phone is ringing off the hook. Everybody wants Big Bird at their parties and events. You even got asked to go to an opera as Big Bird. Why the hell not?
You are very happy and being offered lots of money for attending events. Your calendar is full for the next six months now, but wait, another call from the TV Company.

"Hi there. We have just been looking over the footage again and we have also had a lot of calls into the show asking about Big Bird. We noticed that you are very good in front of the camera, funny and likeable [this is because you are shining and in bliss]. What was also surprising though was your knowledge of sport."

When you were growing up, you went to all the games with your dad. It was your favourite thing to do. You can remember every single one of them.

"Would you be interested in coming back again, this time as yourself though, to do a trial for a slot on the sports roundup, announcing the new events coming up that week?"

"Yes, yes, yes."

Before long you are established as a regular on the show, doing your two favourite things: talking about sport and watching it, and sometimes dressed as a big yellow bird.

You see, by following your dreams and listening to your heart, you fulfil your dharma. You love every day, live in bliss, and now get paid a lot of money from the TV Company. Is this not the better option? Or do you want to go back into that box staring at a computer screen for twelve hours a day? It's a choice!

1. "But this won't actually happen to me."
   Then it will not. Doubt and worry have crept in. You are living in fear and have become a victim of circumstance.

2. "This is definitely going to happen for me."
   Then it will. Now your actions are deliberate and you have become a creator.

Only you can decide. It's up to you. From this point forward, the world you manifest is based solely upon the thoughts that you generate in your mind.

I have listed several quotes next. I have put them together for two reasons. Firstly, because they are all so inspiring, beautiful, and true, but also to labour the point. Using correct thought and then following your dharma is your path to peace. It is such an important lesson to learn. It is crucial to your future happiness. It is pivotal that you understand what is said here, to enable you to experience bliss and joy in every moment, in every single day. Please, you must start to listen to your feelings and follow your heart from here on in.

"If you change the way you look at things, the things you look at change."—Dr Wayne Dyer

"Make a life, not a living."—Dr Wayne Dyer

"If one advances confidently in the direction of his dreams, and endeavours to live the life that he has imagined, he will meet with a success unexpected in common hours."—Henry David Thoreau

"When you are inspired by some great purpose, some extraordinary project, all your thoughts break their bonds: your mind transcends limitations, your consciousness expands in every direction, and you find yourself in a new, great and wonderful world. Dormant forces, faculties, and talents become alive, and you discover yourself to be a greater person by far than you ever dreamed yourself to be."—Patanjali, *The Yoga Sutras of Patanjali*

By the time we leave school, most people usually just want to earn as much money as possible. They want to earn more than anyone else and are prepared to do anything to get it. You are then way out of alignment with your true self and definitely not following your dharma. You are following money and motivated by greed. We are also highly stressed because of exams, academia, and career pressures and are probably so far into debt that we feel lost. You might already have deduced that it's too late, that you will never get back on track and there is no hope. At least that's what they want you to think anyway. Well, that's simply not true. That is just bad programming. Remember, it's never too late. Never!

"When you come to the end of the line, you have to go off the rails."—MM

Your most important job while in this realm is to follow your bliss, spread love, and help others. You only ever have this moment. Start today, right now. Do what you love!

You can do it. You have to be prepared to go back to the drawing board though and make some fundamental changes to the way you think, act, and see the world. To many this can be scary. When you decide to go against your programming it can be very difficult and uncomfortable at first. To do this is to transcend your fears, which are after all, are your thoughts, and therefore born of the mind.

Or you can go the other route, which is not empowering at all and even more frightening, by getting thrown off the treadmill altogether, because it's going so fast that you can't keep up. This can happen by nervous breakdown, midlife crisis or severe illness for example and is usually the start of a spiritual awakening or shift in awareness and the way you see the world. Once you get off it, or thrown off it at speed like me, you regain perspective and you change down gears. You will have an epiphany and be shocked by what you see when you have contrast. The trick is you don't even know you're on the treadmill until you get off it and then stand back and take a good look at your life. It's hard to believe that you have been doing things this way for so long. Things that had been accepted as normal and automatic to you now appear completely alien. Things that afterwards upon reflection make no sense at all and may even seem insane! The human race as a species is generally and on the whole completely insane, by the way, but we will get to that.

The beauty is that once you get off the treadmill and are no longer in the pursuit of material wealth, possessions, and status, you will feel free, liberated, and never want to get back on it again. There's no going back. Once you know something, you can't unknow it. You can't just close your eyes, pretend everything is fine, and go back to your old life, nor will you want too.

Remember, the most important job you have while you are on this earth, in this spacesuit, in this human form we call a body, is to be happy. This may seem selfish at first, but that's just bad programming again. In order to spread love, you must first fill yourself with it. You must first love yourself. You deserve to be happy, you are good enough, you do deserve it and you can do it. Once you are full of love, and meditate, of course, you can then go around spreading peace, and giving joy to all. You can only give out what you have inside. If you are angry inside and you feel the squeeze of a stressful situation, out pops an angry response. If you are peaceful inside and you feel the squeeze of a stressful situation, out pops a peaceful response. So how you feel inside, your inner state, determines how you act, engage, and ultimately influence the outside world. Note that you act, not re-act. The difference between the two involves a small pause and then a choice. Deliberately and intentionally deciding how you behave and respond, rather than being controlled and reacting to external stimulus. Making a choice rather than someone pushing your buttons and manipulating you. Never give this power to someone else. You are after all, the captain of your ship, the master of your destiny and the creator of your universe. Your inner world, that is your thoughts and state of mind, not only dictate your emotional balance and how you feel, but also what you then manifest into the realm of the five senses. As such, your inner state will determine the frequency you emit. This is what you give out to the rest of the universe and hence how you will make everyone else feel around you. The universe is just a great big cosmic mirror.

"We are not human beings having a spiritual experience; we are spiritual beings having a human experience."—Dr Wayne Dyer

FALSE IDOLS

A short note and explanation on "perfection", to clarify.

When I talk about perfection and I say "We are not perfect", I am referring to the fact that we all make mistakes and that we are not perfect as portrayed by the false idols in the media, the perfect that we are programmed to believe we should be by the system, that isn't real. The perfect used in "The Lie".

We are, in fact, all perfect, beings of light created by the divine.

This is our nature. This is the true self. This is the truth.

We are led to believe that there are some people in this world who have perfect lives.

They want for nothing. They live in bliss and never experience any trauma. Now, although these people do exist, they are usually found in monasteries and have no possessions.

"The less you have, the more you see." —MM

This is a deliberate reversal of an earlier quote in the book.

"The more you have, the less you see." —MM

It works both ways.

They are not where you think they are or who they are portrayed to be. They certainly don't live in Hollywood. As always, there are exceptions to every rule. However, I am trying to illustrate a point and therefore not using specific examples.

So, as for the movie stars and pop stars that do live in Hollywood, they don't always have unlimited material wealth, it's an act, and if they do, it doesn't necessarily make them happy. They don't live in bliss, In fact, quite to the contrary. They usually have lots of negative thoughts and emotions like the rest of us, are very unhappy, and aren't always very nice people to be around. They have unhealthy personal relationships, very dysfunctional love lives, and often have substance abuse problems to boot. These are commonplace. Oh, and their pictures are nearly always airbrushed too.

It's all a big flipping lie!

So because of these "false idols", our kids are hardwired for unhappiness. They are all trying to be like people that don't even exist and then they start to feel like they don't fit in, they don't belong, and they aren't good enough. We need to change this nonsense!

These perfect people aren't actually real, at least not as we are led to believe on television and in magazines.

But there is one thing we do all have in common.

"We are all broken, that's how the light gets in."—Ernest Hemingway

It is only through trauma, adversity, and challenge that we learn and grow.

"To appreciate sunlight, first you must stand in the shadows." —MM

Every challenge is an opportunity, if you choose to see it that way.

"It's okay not to be okay. Once you are aware of this, your journey has begun!" —MM

Once we recognise this, we then need to share.

"In order to learn anything, we have to talk about everything." — MM

Without this mantra, we can't encourage other people to open up and talk about their problems. We can't help people if they don't tell us they are suffering. We can't ask for help if we aren't honest with ourselves and others about how we feel and the issues we face. We need to instigate a culture of acceptance and forgiveness, and that it is okay to be human, and it all starts with you. Tell someone about the mistakes you've made. Tell someone about the troubles you've had. Show them that you are vulnerable too. They will probably then relate to your tales and share theirs. You could change the course of someone's life, just by being honest and open with them and not brushing all your mistaken experiences under the carpet. This was the ethos of society in the Edwardian and Victorian periods.

I make mistakes all the time, but I don't beat myself up over them anymore. I do my best and then if things don't go to plan, I just learn from these experiences and try not to take myself too seriously. I'm an idiot! See! I find it helps to laugh at yourself. This softens all the edges.

Frustration is simply a waste of time and very unhelpful. It's a whole new separate mind-created problem, a bad thought pattern that we have inherited, and then repeat. It is when you get mad with yourself or someone else, for not achieving a desired outcome. When we do this, often the secondary mental problem of frustration far outweighs the initial problem or external event. This can all be overcome however with meditation and correct thought.

"To err is human; to forgive, divine."—Alexander Pope

Most people don't realise that this actually starts with you. Inner forgiveness. Be gentle and take it easy on yourself. Forgive yourself first. Then you will be peaceful and surprised, as this makes it a whole lot easier to forgive someone else.

We all make mistakes. This is how we learn. If we don't talk about them however, then we don't share information from the lessons we have learnt and so can't help one another.

We can't make informed decisions to improve the quality of life for everyone if we don't have all the information. We all learn from our experiences if we share them.

In order to grow as a person we have to do new things and step outside our comfort zone, this process includes having lots of problems and making plenty of mistakes. I think from here on in we can just start to call them lessons.

Energy must flow through us. Almost everything in a stagnant pond dies. We need to open the door and let universal energy fill our bodies, rather than resisting it. Working in harmony and operating within natural law, rather than wrestling with it. Taking the path of least resistance.

We need to keep moving forward, mistakes and all!

"You can't fight water, but you can bathe in it."—MM

THE MEDIA

Firstly, there is one very important fact to take note of here. You need to constantly remind yourself that the media is a business. Any business normally has one primary goal, and that is to make money. The media is no exception to this rule. It consists of lots of different companies and corporations, and their motivations are usually one of three things:

1. **To make money (to sell you stuff).**

2. **To manipulate and control you through fear (to sell you more stuff).**

3. **To promote a political agenda using propaganda (to control and manipulate you through fear).**

    You see, no matter how you look at it, it always comes back to money. Every time. Most humans have an unquenchable thirst and craving for money. These financial desires are the self imposed shackles of modern slavery.

Usually all three listed above are connected. The unholy trinity, if you will.
They have a common theme and a collective goal. Primarily, to control your decision-making process by pumping out fear on the news, then to sell you stuff like Big Pharma that you don't really need, and finally to promote a political agenda such as

war. Oil is usually why we go to war anyway. If not, then for the control of the surrounding regions of the oil-rich nations. So the media is promoting drugs, war, and oil, three of the biggest industries on the planet. They want us to agree to go to work and pay our taxes to finance the war machine. They want us to think that we are under threat, buying more stuff we don't need to distract ourselves from our true nature, and then taking drugs we also don't need to help us cope, the whole time living in fear. This is "The Lie".

> Try this on for size. Did you know that statins are now the biggest selling drug of all time and, in most cases, taken just in case? It's a massive marketing scam: selling drugs to people that don't need them. Yes, some people do actually benefit from them, but on the whole, they are now being prescribed as a precautionary measure. A drug we take to prevent us getting ill. They have raised the bar here. Drugs don't usually solve the problem anyway, they just alleviate it temporarily, but what if we are not even ill? This is genius. Big Pharma still not being happy wanted to sell us more of the drugs that we didn't need, so what did they do? It gets worse. One of the biggest cons of all time. Pfizer, the world's largest research-based pharmaceutical company, manufactured the drug Lipitor. This was the most widely used and biggest-selling drug of its type, part of the category or classification known as statins. A huge fear-based marketing campaign, called "Know Your Number", was launched. Direct prescription pharmaceutical advertising is still legal in the States. The idea was that

if you kept your cholesterol count low, you could avoid heart disease, high cholesterol being one of many possible factors that contributes to this and others heart related issues. Eligibility in America at the time was determined from guidelines set by the committee at the National Institute of Health. These figures determined if your cholesterol count was considered too high, and thus if you were at risk and needed to take statins. It is very common for the people on these boards and councils to be financially connected in some way to the companies who make the drugs and that benefit from their advice (for example, ex-employees of a pharmaceutical company who are now on the board of directors or committees of another beneficiary company) There are massive conflicts of interest in Big Pharma and corruption is rife. Six of the seven members on the committee who were involved in making the decision to lower the cholesterol threshold, and hence put someone on the at-risk register, had financial ties with Pfizer, the company who manufactured the drug. Overnight, the number of people who fell into the category to be prescribed statins almost tripled. It went from thirteen to thirty-six million people. So if you had a medium cholesterol count on a Tuesday and you were not at risk, you went to bed and while you were sleeping everything changed. You woke up the next morning to find that you were classed as having a high cholesterol count, and you were also now on the at-risk register and hence prescribed statins. Another twenty-three million people were now on the drug, and these are just the statistics for America. This actually happened, folks.

Nothing actually changed and yet, from one decision, millions of people got given a drug they did not need. It is fraud, plain and simple.

Don't get me started on "planned obsolescence"!

Please watch *The Men Who Made Us Spend*. This is a three-part BBC documentary on consumerism. It's fascinating. The statistics I refer to are in episode two.

For some reason, we think that if we are in a cinema we are watching a movie, but if we turn on a television what we are witnessing is the truth and real. If you open your eyes, you will see that we are being manipulated and controlled by the media, using fear on a global scale.

I have seen this first-hand. I have watched the news on two different news channels in two different countries during a conflict between them. They were in complete disagreement. The channels reported completely different stories and wildly varying facts about the events to the people in the respective countries. This is because it's not news. It's propaganda designed for the masses, both governments and the media corporations are biased. They even have corroborating video footage. Somebody's lying! The facts are the facts. They both have an agenda, hidden political and financial motivations. What is worse is that some very serious events that have occurred aren't even reported at all.

There is no "good news"! It's all negative. Constantly streaming out of our televisions, into our living rooms and bedrooms, into our homes. Until we become enlightened beings, we will still be affected by our environment, so we need to choose very carefully what we allow to pervade into our energy fields and hence into our lives.

Turn the TV off!

In fact, you don't need to go abroad to see this. Just look in the newspapers here. Two newspapers can tell two completely different versions of the same event. They are politically motivated. It's not even a secret.

Oh yes, and lastly, I can recall when Tony Blair faced questioning as part of the Chilcot enquiry. It was his first day to participate in the proceedings and his turn to take the stand. He was to be questioned on our nation's role in the Iraq War. A pretty big news story, you might think. The story barely made the papers at all. Page ten in a tiny article was their best effort. Instead, they led with John Terry and his affair with a woman who was managed by Max Clifford. The papers later admitted that they had known about this story for months. It was on the front page of every tabloid, and there was the small matter of two hundred thousand people dying in an earthquake in Haiti at the same time, which didn't receive due diligence either. These are manipulation and diversion tactics, those used by magicians and masters of illusion. This is not news people. It is in fact calculated deception!

"As long as there are us and them, you can't have zen!" —MM

"More fighting never solved a war. Only peace can dissolve conflict." —MM

"WAR"

WAR

So, to war. This is probably the biggest business on the planet. It is at the very top of the supply chain for several of the largest and most expensive manufacturing industries known to mankind. Think of submarines, fighter jets, aircraft carriers, and military helicopters. It is directly connected to many other industries that supply it and knowingly benefit from it, but also to thousands of other smaller industries that indirectly feed it and perhaps unwittingly depend upon it. As things stand half of the Western world would go bankrupt if we were not constantly at war. Think guns, missiles, bombs, tanks, airplanes, warships, computers, construction, uniforms, food, etc. This small list is just a taster, to give you an idea of how huge the cogs of this machine really are. At first glance, you see only a fragment of what is actually involved, but the more you look into it and start to join the dots, the more you become aware of the massive zone of influence of this well-oiled machine. It is totally mind-boggling. In America, for example, a large number of senators and congressmen are also shareholders or on the board of directors for many of the major companies that supply the troops. They all profit to the tune of millions from the war machine. Just look at Dick Cheney and Halliburton. Here in England, this would be illegal and seen as a conflict of interest. They have a large monetary stake and a deeply vested financial motivation in keeping the wheels of this machine turning, staying in conflicts across the globe. It's very hard to swallow when you look at it with your eyes wide open. The decisions they make, passing new bills and laws, directly affect their bank balances. This is a criminal affair. Blood is their hallmark and death is their currency.

Make no mistake; war is very big business indeed! They are peddling propaganda and selling us lies in order to get us to agree to invade other countries, in the name of freedom and to "liberate the people". This is nonsense, of course. The reality is that most of the casualties in modern warfare are civilian. We go into a country and take all of the natural resources by means of murder, torture, and the taking of civil liberties, and this is usually after imposing economic sanctions. All of this is for the purposes of control and financial gain, definitely not for liberation. More often than not, it is for oil. We are like the Vikings "pillaging and plundering" other countries, just a little less honest about it. This is as far away as we could possibly be from our true nature, from natural law, from harmony.

"War is complete madness. It is insanity personified. No exception!"—MM

The Iraq War death toll:

British soldier deaths	179
American solider deaths	4,486
Iraqi deaths	500,000 +

Various sources report wildly different figures about Iraqi civilian casualties, but the lowest is 165,000 and the highest is at 600,000.

YOUNG MEN

Well, they don't mess about here. They start to programme us from a very early age, right from the beginning. Giving young children toys that mimic actual weapons, designed to kill people. Can you see how insane this is? I mean, who hasn't had a toy gun? Maybe a toy tank? Or a toy soldier? A G.I. Joe, maybe? Both of these, "toy soldiers" and "G.I Joe", have now been made into Hollywood blockbuster movies, specifically created for the viewing pleasure of our young ones. They want us to start seeing war as completely normal and to think that being a soldier is cool. The A-Team shooting automatic weapons on TV at three in the afternoon has become completely acceptable. God forbid we see a vagina! Part of the human body that is perfectly designed by nature.

Maybe we're taking our kids out for a fun day trip to go and watch the Navy. A new aircraft carrier, or "destroyer", is being launched, sailing past in the local harbour? Possibly waving a flag, full of pride as it goes past? Open your eyes: this is a killing machine, a war ship. The US Navy's Nimitz class aircraft carriers, for example, weighing in at more than 100,000 tons of metal each. They are up to 330 metres long, can house a crew of up to 5,000, and carry more than 70 fighter jets. A floating bringer of death, that takes years to build and is specifically designed to kill humans en masse with large guns, rockets, and bombs. Oh, and the cost of this is about nine billion dollars per unit. I will have ten, please! This is the definition of insanity right here. Some kids don't even have food or clothes! What chance do they have? I mean both the kids being brainwashed and the opposing side.

You see, they start very young and come at you from every angle. My idols as a kid were all tough men. Sylvester Stallone, Arnold Schwarzenegger, Hulk Hogan, and Bruce Lee too, although he did have some very wise philosophies and he wasn't on testosterone.

"Those who are unaware they are walking in darkness will never seek the light."—Bruce Lee

You see, with the exception of Bruce Lee, all these guys were pumped up on steroids. This fact, however, doesn't trouble me at all and it is no secret now anyway; they have all since admitted it. So it's not the steroids that were the problem, it was the lies, the false idols they portrayed in the media, the ideals and values they represented. I haven't met any of them yet myself, and I am sure they are all lovely men in person, but they each played characters that were full of macho nonsense. They responded to every situation with aggression, and dealt out violence to everyone they encountered. This programming, along with lots of other sources at the time, led me to think that this was acceptable behaviour. It took me many years to figure out that violence was an incorrect form of expression and that anger wasn't a good emotion to carry around with you. I was led to believe that the characters they played were real men. Real men! I don't think so.

"The harder the shell, the easier it cracks!"—MM

A real man is someone who is wise and expresses himself without hurting others, and who improves the lives of all the people around him. I now admire quiet, gentle men who don't need to tell everyone how tough they are.

"An eye for an eye only ends up making the whole world blind."—M. Gandhi

So you're in your teens and you're a man now, right? You're ready to fight? There is a good reason why men over the age of thirty-three aren't required in the British army. They are a lot harder to programme. They want young men, as young as they can get them without causing a national outrage. Believe it or not, in this country you can still enlist into the British Army at just fifteen years of age. You're not old enough to vote yet, you're not old enough to make love, you can't drink or drive either, and you're three years away from buying your first packet of cigarettes, but you can join the army. An institution that trains you how to kill other human beings. Yes, that is fine. That is total madness!

In the past, we have knowingly sent thousands of underage boys to war. Can you imagine? It is hard to comprehend.

250,000 boys between the ages of 14 and 18 served in the British Army during World War One. The youngest was found to be just 12. The average life expectancy in the trenches was just six weeks. They were sent off to almost certain death.

Can you imagine a load of fourteen-year-old boys wanting to take their driving test early, trying to sneak into the line with fake IDs? They wouldn't have a chance, but sending them to war was deemed acceptable and everyone turned a blind eye.

By the way, when was the last time you saw a seventy-year-old suicide bomber?

I hazard a guess that the answer is never!

I mean, all they have to do is put on a vest, right? Do you think maybe it's because they don't want to die? They know it's all a lie and so they target young men to do it instead. They start by brainwashing them, by selling religion and martyrdom to these boys. Eventually, they manage to convince these poor souls to sacrifice their lives, to do their dirty work for them, masking the real hidden agenda. No one should ever have to give up their life for someone else's motivations. Your life is your own.

So it is not because younger men are fitter, as we are usually told, although this is generally true of course and hence a great cover story, but because most men, by the time they reach the age of forty, would point blank refuse to go to war. They would not put on the uniform and certainly wouldn't be prepared to kill anyone, for that matter. A lot of young men are also very angry and haven't yet figured out that it is okay to express your emotions, or how to actually do it.

"Don't be so soft, son!"

You see, young men, far from being the strongest, are actually some of the most easily influenced and vulnerable members of our society. Have you seen the adverts on TV for the army?

You get to travel all over the world and make new friends and it builds your character. What an adventure? I mean, you would think it was just one big holiday. There is no mention of the fact that you will probably have to kill people on your holiday, or that you will see things that could do irreparable damage to your mind. If you do make it home, possibly with a limb missing, you will realise it was all lies and then you will likely suffer from mental health problems like PTSD. That wouldn't make such a good advert, would it? I don't think the armed forces should ever be allowed to advertise. We have a warning on every packet of cigarettes, for God's sake, and yet they are still getting away with this drivel. This is false advertising and quite simply pure fiction.

Do you know that more US troops committed suicide after they returned home from Iraq and Afghanistan than were actually killed in combat?

Did you know that at least 30% of all these troops developed mental health problems within three months of arriving home?

That fact alone should tell you everything you need to know about war! It's insane and directly opposite to the inner voice that is the true self, our true nature, born from peace and love. It's travelling in a speedboat at full throttle against the current and flow of universal energy. It is an affront to natural law.

Imagine being inside the head of a young man. After being conditioned, you don't know how to express yourself well and you're probably angry. Then you're instilled with a false sense of national pride and told that you have to look after your own first, to defend your country and family from foreign threats, and also told that if you don't then go to war, you're a coward. What would you do? I would probably go to war with the best intentions and motivations, believing I was doing the right thing. It's ridiculous!

As for national service, it is basically forcing people to fight against their will. It should be abolished by using the Human Rights Act. What about free will? It's akin to slavery! If you joined a gang and then killed for their agenda, it would be categorical murder.

As with everything, there are of course exceptions to the rule, but generally speaking, a spiritual awakening or shift comes with age.

It can be very scary when you first realise that everything you have been told is a lie and that everything you think you know is wrong. It can rock you down to your foundations. You realise that every decision you have ever made and are making, right now even, is incorrect, based on lies, and that a large proportion of what you have done with your life is meaningless. Then you start to ask the question what is the point? But don't worry, there is one!

Remember, "You can't build the truth on a lie."—MM

There is a reason why the biggest killer of men under the age of forty in this country is suicide. This is due to bad programming, to them not expressing themselves and also developing a false self. This is called the ego and in most cases, for men, full of macho rubbish. We have to start learning how to express ourselves, and that it's not "soft" to be emotional, to show love to another man, or to enjoy painting pictures or writing poems.

This is not to disrespect any young people who have been in the armed services or are in a war zone or conflict at the moment. They usually do this with all the right intentions, with the motivation to protect their families and country. This is very "honourable". However, the fact is that most of the time, the information they were fed to get them to do this was false and the threat wasn't even real. If there is a real threat, it is usually as a result of atrocities we have committed first and that we are not shown in the media here. Often, the conflicts across the world are fed by weapons which we have manufactured and then have sold to both sides. Yes, that's right, we have a history of selling weapons to countries that we later go to war with. After all, the war machine doesn't work if there is nobody to fight with. These other nations are also being manipulated and lied to in this whole mess. Their young men are responding to protect their countries and families from a threat too. Remember, this is "honourable", right? It's just that usually in their case, the threat and actions taken against them are actually genuine!

When I say "we" or "us" in this instance, I refer to America and the UK, with France right up there in the mix too. France has a long unusual history in wars, of being involved with conflicts within the African nations. Does this not seem quite odd to you? Why no help in Rwanda then? Do you think that France has a particular soft spot for certain African nations? Or do you think that it's really about money and oil?

I have several good friends who are ex-soldiers and who I don't wish to offend. I love them dearly and respect them. I just think that conflict is not the answer. The wars we are fighting are over money and oil, not safety.

"Just like pouring gasoline onto a fire, more fighting never solved a war."—MM

This next point I am going to make is what I call "Hero/Murderer/Terrorist":

1. A Hero—someone who kills for the political agenda of our government or body (usually in very large numbers).
2. A Murderer—someone who kills for their own agenda (usually one person at a time).
3. A Terrorist—someone who kills for the political agenda of an opposing government or body (usually in large numbers).

The actual definition of a terrorist is "someone who instils terror" and yes, that includes us folks! Now, murder is unacceptable in all its forms—no exception! The individual murder of one human being by another usually happens when someone experiences extreme emotional anguish, perhaps mental health problems, or sometimes unfortunately for financial gain. Now look at the definition of a hero and that of a terrorist. There is no difference between them except for their agenda. Their motivation is simply different, that of the government that they are killing for. A matter of opinion, you might say. Okay, the weapons may vary, but that is just down to the means available to them at the time. You see, our heroes are another country's terrorists, and vice versa. A response I hear a lot to this is that "terrorists target civilians, but we target soldiers".

Well, that simply isn't true. I have three points to make here.

1. Please! You have to see with better eyes: this is a lie. Check out the civilian casualty statistics for Iraq, Afghanistan, and Syria.
2. There are a lot of atrocities that don't make the headlines over here. America, the UK, and France are some of the biggest terrorists on the planet.
The US has hit three hospitals in recent years, for example. Directly in Iraq and Afghanistan, and then a third by US-backed rebel groups in Syria. One in each of the above conflicts. So we have the technology to pinpoint a missile strike to within the size of a postage stamp, but we blew up the wrong buildings? Wrong target! What a load of rubbish! There are only three examples listed here. There are many more. If they continue to kill the families of people in other countries, they will keep fighting back, and of course this is what they want. This is the war machine in action, in full swing. As you now know, war is very big business, and the cost is too high, carnage and human suffering.

"Fear a man who fears no consequence!"—MM

When you take away everyone that they love, then they have nothing left to lose.

3. All life is equal. Yes, it may be more upsetting to see a child die than an adult. I concur and sign up to this, but all life is precious and should be treated as such. A British life is no more valuable than a Syrian life or an American life.
All life is equal! There is only one race, and that is the human race.

As a Buddhist, I believe that all life is sacred. I will never willingly kill any living thing! Imagine tomorrow, if we all decided never to kill anyone again on someone else's behalf. There would be no more war! Refuse to fight. It's not in our nature anyway. Don't let them fool you. Don't put on a uniform! We could get the same result by everyone in the world learning how to meditate and we could all develop inner peace. You can only give what you have inside, remember. For some strange reason, you tell someone to put on a uniform and suddenly they think it is okay to kill people? Give them a false sense of pride, power, and a sense of threat or impending doom and hey presto—you've got yourself an army! They use national pride, group identity, group ego, and fear to justify their actions and motivate people. How to Get Oil 101? Attack! What a great way to respond to a non-existent threat! Think I'm joking? Just think Iraq and WMDs.

Dr David Kelly spoke out about our plans to invade Iraq under false pretences, which was highly inconvenient, and he was then found dead two days later. He had been nominated for a Nobel Peace Prize. He was a top weapons expert and yet apparently took his own life with "a blunt garden knife". Lord Hutton tried to suppress the release of the post mortem for seventy years with a secrecy order, to "protect the family". No one in the history of man has ever bled to death from severing their ulnar artery. It's physically impossible because it is simply too small. Oh, and did I mention that there were no fingerprints found on the knife. I can smell something. What is it? Ah yes, that's it, unmistakable, bull poo!

Anyway, I think it's time we prepared to leave "The Lie" now. You see, in order to control people, governments and countries need to divide and conquer. To fragment the people, creating separation and then conflict. If we all acted as one and loved each other, there would be no wars and no way to control us. Alone, we are like a single drop of water and have little strength, but together we have great power like the oceans and can move mountains.

Universe

Uni-Verse

One-Song

I could go on and on but as you can see, it's very easy to get lost in "The Lie".

Other topics would include technology, religion, and consumerism.

This first part of my book was the hardest to write. I had to spend a long time looking at what is wrong with the human race. I am glad it's over. Ironically, I spend all my time talking about inner peace and harmony now, which is what we are going to focus on from here on in. You have made it over the hill. Well done, the ride will get a whole lot easier from here on in. We visited here so we could gain perspective and understanding only, but we don't want to dwell or live here. Now let's get out of "The Lie". Let's focus on were we go from here.

"But where do we go now?"

"Let's move towards love!"

Not One of Us

How can I kill, let me count the ways, in darkest night and blood soaked days.

In the name of righteousness indeed, or political power, or human greed.

I can kill with hate or intolerance; I can kill with a minimum of fuss.

I can kill for any such reason, but I kill 'cos you're not one of us.

You're not a member of my tribe; you don't have the same God as me,

Although you're a member of the human race, it's beyond my wish to see.

That a day may dawn on planet earth that brings peace for you and me,

But the distance between our cultures mean; it's simply not to be.

I beat you 'cos I have the power, I have the troops on my side.

I kill you 'cos I have the gun, not because it's genocide.

I hate you 'cos you're one of them, not just because I must,

And you hate me respectively, 'cos you're not one of us.

So human rights don't make me wrong, that's not my point of view

Asserting the balance of power again, is what, we're trying to do.

Last week you tried to kill my friend, and it changed his point of view,

So he's become a renegade and now he's one of you.

But you're never going to win the fight; we'll grind you to the dust,

And drive you from our blessed land, 'cos you're not one of us.

Now the distance that lies between us, need not be measured in miles,

But perhaps in man's inability to understand different styles.

Of religious beliefs and cultures, in all the dream is one

But in man's continued advancement so little have we done.

To close the distance between us, between the 'have's' and 'have not'

With greed and possession becoming the norm, so much has man forgot

Don't ask for ways of knowing, just accept that we're all one

And bridge the gulf between us and the human race is won.

A poem by my friend, D.W. Parry.

"The further down you start, the more remarkable your journey." —MM

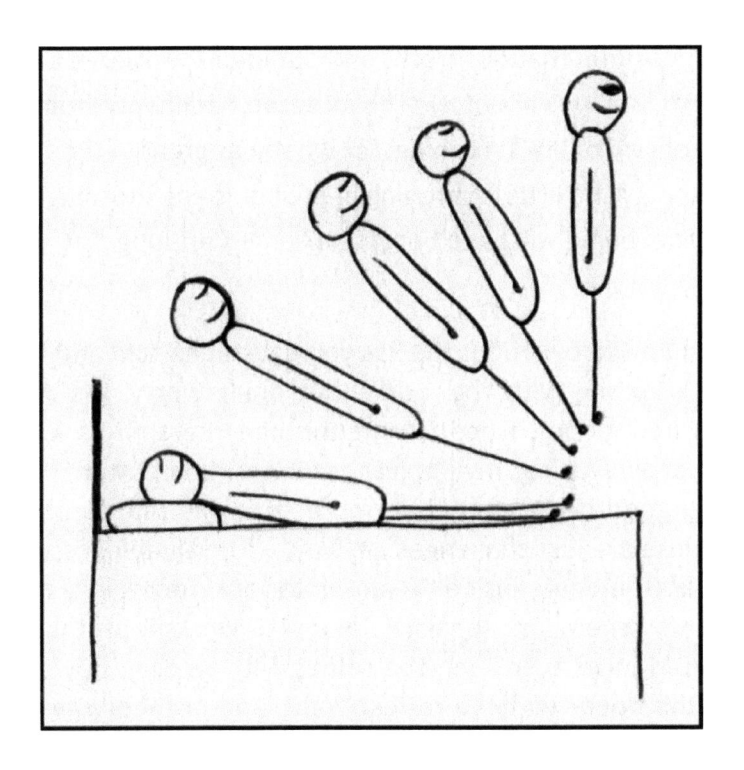

"AWAKENING"

3. AWAKENING

"Thoroughly unprepared, we take the step into the afternoon of life. Worse still, we take this step with the false presupposition that our truths and our ideals will serve us as hitherto. But we cannot live the afternoon of life according to the program of life's morning, for what was great in the morning will be little at evening and what in the morning was true, at evening will have become a lie."—Carl Jung

So you now know about the lies you have been told and hence what is wrong with the world, but don't worry, it's not all doom and gloom. Once I went through the shift, a kind of spiritual awakening, my life just got better and better. There's mainly good news after that, more solutions than problems, and these are just challenges anyway, with valuable lessons to be learnt hidden inside. I am notorious for going off on tangents when I'm speaking. No two workshops that I've delivered have ever been the same. With writing, however, I have the opportunity to re-read, edit, and in theory get back on track. However, I still love going off plan and just letting it flow, so most of the tangents remain.

MY STORY

So now let's get to the bones of it. Where to begin my story? Although I believe in being completely open and honest, I also believe in people's right to privacy and I respect that. So for this reason I will keep the names out of most of my stories. I also don't want to cause any unnecessary hurt, to my family for example, so I will spare some of the details of my hedonistic past.

However, if I have the pleasure of meeting you in person at some point in the future, or if you already know me and have been to one of my talks, you will know that there are no holds barred. I will happily let rip with stories that will make your hair stand on end, but again, never discussing anyone's name unless it is appropriate to do so.

Remember, "In order to learn anything, we have to talk about everything."—MM

You can't make informed decisions and good choices without all the facts.

Since I was a young child, I have always been fascinated by the mind. I remember watching the movie *Poltergeist* as a child and being terrified. Believe it or not, there was even an episode of *The Waltons* all about poltergeists and possession. I don't mean a light-hearted look at tables and chairs moving around the room that turned out to be a hoax or something else. No, I mean one of the girls in the show was actually possessed, and for this reason it was put on TV later than usual. It properly messed me up. Imagine Daffy Duck shooting up heroin with kids watching. You get the idea; it was disturbing. I remember watching *Star Wars* for the first time and then spending hours using "The Force", trying to move objects with my mind, a pursuit I still regularly practice to this day. Now, if I were to say, "The Force is strong in this one" or "Young Padawan", this refers to one person in particular, and you know who you are! My former apprentice in the dark arts and my pupil from our hedonistic past, who has since become the master. Just sharing my sense of humour with you here. Actually, it's one of my dearest friends. I since learned, however, that I can move objects with my mind. Using intelligence, good manners and respect. Asking someone for help if required, to move the objects on my behalf. It's not cheating really. It is still moving objects using the power of my mind!

In my teens I tried every technique, anything available to me at the time, to explore the mind. I was fascinated by this field of study and so anything I could find that excited my brain, I read up on it first and then off I went. An astronaut of the spirit or true self, exploring my consciousness. Consequently, I went through a whole array of experiences and emotions as you can imagine.

This following list is to name but a few:

Self-hypnosis
Astral projection
Out of body experiences
Visiting the spirit realm

Anger
Violence
Depression
Possession
Speed writing
Channelling

Although some of these may seem a bit way out there and ridiculous to you at first, when the door is open, you can see outside the electromagnetic spectrum. You see with different eyes. I can assure you that they are all very real phenomenon and that they all actually happened. Either that or everyone will think I'm mental. No change there then. This was before I really started to explore the world of drugs in depth. I think at this point I had only really taken cannabis and maybe some LSD.
In my later teens I was fascinated by drugs and their effects on the mind and wanted to explore them. I think at last count I have taken over thirty different types of drugs, and that's just the illegal ones. If I was to say that during my time on this planet there were three fields that I could claim to be an expert in, three matters that I was very well-versed and experienced in, those specialised areas would be Meditation, Drugs, and Civil Engineering. If I was on *Mastermind*, they would be my chosen subjects. This is where this part of my story ends for now however, just to spare my friends and family any pain.
To be clear, I am in no way encouraging anyone to take drugs. I now know that there are far better and less destructive ways to find peace, quiet the mind and expand your consciousness. Drugs are definitely not the answer, but they were however, a big part of my journey.

There are a couple of quotes I would like to share with you now. Ironically, I actually wrote both of them from a spiritual perspective for this book, but in writing this chapter, I now find them hilarious, far too funny to keep to myself. It's very important not to take yourself too seriously and to be able to laugh at yourself.

"In order to see what lies beneath, we need to get high!"—MM

"The higher you get, the more you can see."—MM

So I did a degree in Construction at Sheffield Hallam University. Then, once I had finished, I went straight out and got the highest paid job I could. Now, up until this point, any careers that I had shown an interest in that weren't financially lucrative were quashed immediately. Those dreams had no place in this material world. If it wasn't going to make me a lot of cash then it wasn't even on the table. I was told that money was everything and that you should start to acquire as much of it as possible as soon as you can. It was like an insane race without a finish line, except for death of course. I had been conditioned that this was how you were judged by society and that this was the mark of being a true success. The more flashy material stuff you had, the greater the person you were. That appearances and the impression you made on everyone else, actually mattered and was very important. Clearly, this was all nonsense of course, but when you're young you are easily programmed.

So I ended up going into the world of construction, made lots of money for a young man, and was very "successful" at it, but I was miserable. Consequently, I started to develop very unhealthy coping mechanisms. These obviously included drugs and alcohol.

I was then no longer exploring higher levels of consciousness and the unlimited expanses of the mind; this was now using chemicals as a crutch to help me manage stress.

"Drink when you want to remember, don't drink when you want to forget, but remember, sobriety improves society."—MM

You see, I wasn't having fun, although I thought I was at the time. It felt good because I was comfortably numb. Now, with perspective and balance, everything is very clear to me.

"If you want to bathe in the light, you must first know the dark."—MM

"When the sea is rough and the waves are high, you can't see land. But when the sea is calm and still, you can navigate with your vision."—MM

I am not talking about seeing with your eyes here. When your mind is still you can navigate with your inner vision, from within.

I like this analogy.

When the river is busy you can't see below the water. The sediment is getting washed around and it's very cloudy. When the river is still, however, the sediment falls to the bottom, your vision improves, and you can see the river bed. You can see clearly now.
This is much like the human mind and our thoughts within it. Through meditation, by quieting the mind, going into the gap between thoughts and becoming still, you develop inner peace and then have great mental clarity. You also gain perspective and focus.

I was trying to turn my mind off using chemicals, because I didn't know any other way.
If I had known then what I know now about meditation, maybe I wouldn't have gone through as much suffering, but then again, it's only through adversity and facing our fears that we really learn life's lessons. We learn this experientially, by knowing.
So in order for me to be here now, to know what I know, and to write this book, I had to be there then, to experience the suffering. It's a funny old world, isn't it?

"When you are in the dark and you look around, you can see the light very clearly; do you have the courage to follow it? You have to move through the darkness to reach it. To transcend fear. That's where the answers lie. That's where you will find the truth. Everything you are seeking lies on the other side, waiting for you. It's always been there!" —MM

It can take many years to find your true path, your calling, or your dharma, and some people never find it. If, however, you slow down and start to look around, the signs are everywhere. This is your journey. The path you must follow and the lessons you must learn are your own.

"Maktub!"—*The Alchemist* by Paulo Coelho (meaning "It is written")

So I wasn't having much fun, to be honest. These days I just try to remember the good bits and focus on the positives. For example, I still have some wonderful lifelong friends from this period. They were part of my life before I went through the process of spiritual awakening. However, I have also made lots of new friends on my journey, including some nuns and monks. It's not that I have any issues with all my old friends or that I don't love them, it's just that in order to survive, I had to try to cultivate a healthier environment for myself. In doing this, I needed to be alone for a while. I realised that I was starting to think differently and I didn't want to repeat the same patterns again and again. I desperately wanted to change my lifestyle and in order to do this; I first needed to change my surroundings. I had decided that I didn't want to do the same things anymore and that I had had enough.

"When patterns are broken, new worlds emerge."—Tuli Kupferberg

For example, it is very rare I set foot in a pub these days and I haven't watched a game of football in many years. I would rather stick a fork in my eye. So just by abstaining from these two activities, drinking and football, the commonalities between me and about 95% of my old group of friends have been removed. I did invite all my friends and family to attend the Buddhist temple on my birthday three years ago. Although many of my family members came, as yet only one of my male friends has been to Manjushri with me.

Thanks, George. I'm sure he won't mind a mention in this respect.

Manjushri is the New Kadampa Buddhist Centre in Ulverston. I call this my spiritual home. This is where I have spent many months, in total, on retreat.

One of the many huge positives I've found since I started practicing meditation, and hence teaching it and giving talks, is that I have met a whole new set of people along the way, my spiritual friends and family. You see, it is never really about the destination. If you just focus on that, you will miss the ride. It is the journey that matters. The experiences you have, the lessons you learn and the people you meet and maybe even try to help. It's about the good deeds you do and the opportunities you are given as you go along your path. If you are able to help others, it is a great form of therapy and self-healing.

"Through charity, comes clarity." —MM

Ah yes, so I was trying to switch off my mind. This was because it was so busy and it wasn't functioning very well. I had many recurring, incorrect and negative thought patterns. There was a host of inner problems I needed to address.

1. Dis–ease (This is anxiety, worry, and an unhappy balance inside that can cause disease and illness.)

2. Im-balance (This is where "I" am more important than everyone else and the ego is in charge instead of listening to my true nature. The balance of power lies with the false self.)

3. Dis-chord (This is when the door is closed and your connection to the un-manifest is cut. You could also call this the unified field, the intelligent system, the spirit realm, or God, if you will. Either way, the link to the creator has been lost, and at least temporarily, the chord has been severed.)

The way I was feeling inside did not correspond in any way to my actions outside. They were way out of alignment. This was due to how I had been conditioned and bad programming.
This went on for many years, decades even. The sadness just got worse and the partying was directly proportional to this. The worse I felt, the harder I partied. Then it wasn't really what you could call partying at all anymore, it was self-harm, a destructive force.
You get the picture. I will leave it there.

"The music you hear inside is your dharma. Dance to it!" —MM

A quote for my friend Ash, he is the greatest dancer.

"If you want your life to flow, you have to let it all go." —MM

"MY AWAKENING"

MY AWAKENING

Do you remember being a child, putting your fingers in your ears and going "I'm not listening! La la la la la..."? Effectively being in la la land.
Well, it's no different to what we now do as adults. We don't want to face the fear and go against our programming. We create constant distractions and lots of mental noise to avoid this process, such as watching television, going shopping, and playing on computer games. We do this so that we don't have to go inward, into the silence, and deal with the fact that most of us don't fit into this mad house, and that we are all actually on the whole miserable. Oh, and that we are all dying too. By the way, just a quick note here, nobody ever actually dies. You simply transcend this physical form. Your spirit, that is your true self, constantly moves in and out of form, between different realms. So we subconsciously tell ourselves that there is nothing wrong and we think that ignorance is bliss. Once you're awake however, you reconnect with your true nature, you remember that you are a divine being and that you have unlimited potential, and then you see the world as it really is. There is no turning around at this point. You can never go back, and you won't want to either.
I can hear what you're thinking, so just a couple of points to clear up here:

1. Yes, we do have to go shopping sometimes, but only to provide the essentials, things like food, clothes, and shelter. Consumerism as a form of diversion and distraction is very unhealthy and usually leads to

financial problems and debt, which can create a lot of unnecessary stress.

2. Yes, there are some great documentaries on TV, but soaps, the news, and violent films are full of negative energy and are definitely not good for the soul. Try and reduce the amount of television you watch. It's just a bad habit. Also, if you must, try and pick your programmes carefully, avoiding the advertisements, or just leaving the TV on in the background. Certainly not watching it as you go to bed and fall asleep. I have heard some people say that they just leave it on for company; well, this isn't good company and it is unwittingly brainwashing you.

3. Yes, we all need computers, but we don't need violent computer games for our kids because it keeps them quiet, nor do we need social media twenty-four hours a day until we end up becoming addicted to it. There is an incredible planet of diversity out there waiting to be explored and there is an amazing unlimited world inside just waiting to be seen. This world of pure peace and bliss is in every single one of us, if only we took the time and learned how to tap into it. So keep computer usage and contact to a minimum. They reduce your interaction with other people and the outside world, they prevent you from having emotional exchanges and developing relationships, and they deplete your energy levels and diminish your spirit.

So I was very unhappy and felt like I was slowly dying inside, until one day everything changed. It happened to me. My computer broke, if you will. There was a virus in my software and it had shut down completely. The system crashed and I could not function. Something was seriously wrong. I literally couldn't get out of bed. I had anxiety, panic attacks, no energy, and couldn't even face going outside. I definitely didn't want to be around people. I went through a spiritual awakening, or "the shift". You might want to call it a nervous breakdown, although apparently this is not a recognised medical term. Not me. I couldn't even say this phrase out loud until about a year later, because of the stigma attached to it. Imagine being unwell but not being able to tell anyone about it because you were worried about what they might say or think. The term I decided to go with when I was first able to talk about it some months later was "a wobble". Yes, I'd had "a bit of a wobble".

"If you keep saying "obl", you're going to have a wobble!" — MM

Obligated

Obliged

Obligates

Obligation

Oblong

"If your motivations are born out of obligation, they are someone else's, not yours. You are following their wishes, not your dharma." —MM

Even being as ill as I was, I refused any kind of help or therapy because of my stupid pride, and also because of the fear of being judged by other people, that had been instilled into me. This was a slow process anyway. There was a waiting list and it would have taken about four months before I could even get an appointment and be seen by someone. In the end, after about a year, I did have two sessions of counselling and they did not help one bit, but I don't think this was the fault of the therapist. I simply wasn't able to share or willing to open up at this point. I think that in order for therapy or counselling to be effective, you need a lot of it, on a frequent basis, with the same person, and it needs to be sustained. For me personally, it also had to be with someone who had lived it. For example, the best drug councillors are ex-drug users, not degree students fresh from university, although their intentions may be pure. I know lots of people who have benefitted from counselling, just not me. Like I said, I don't think I was a very willing participant at that time. I would cover my face when I went into the health centre, frightened of being seen by someone I knew.

On a tangent here:

This reminds me of going into the STD clinic at Bolton hospital and bumping into a friend of mine in the waiting room. We laughed about it; we had to, and there was nowhere to hide. Admit it: we've all been there in our youth and there is no shame in it.

I also used to frequent the Buddhist centre in Bolton for a little while. I hadn't really told anyone about it at that point. I used to take some ridiculous route through the town centre to get to the front door, avoiding anywhere that I might come across people I knew. I was very well-known at the time for all the wrong reasons and friendly with lots of people in the area. I was particularly terrified of seeing any of the doormen as I passed the pubs and clubs, in case they saw me go inside. They all knew me because I used to party with them. I imagined them saying things like "He's gone soft", "We always knew he was mental", and "He's a pussy". Back then, this stuff actually mattered to me. It also turns out that they didn't say those things anyway. These were just my thoughts, mind created fears. Well, except the one that I was mental, there is no debating that. They said that way before I had "a wobble". "The Force" was always strong in this one.

"All anyone ever wants is peace, even if they don't know it yet." —MM

"GOOD MENTAL HEALTH"

GOOD MENTAL HEALTH

Did you know that one in four people experience mental health issues at some point in their life? Yes? I think most of us have heard this statistic by now, right?

The actual statistic is very different.

One in four people in the UK will experience a mental health problem "each year".

If you read these statistics carefully, they paint a very different picture. One in four people each year. Well, if I live until I am eighty, for example, and I have a mental health issue every four years, that's twenty episodes in my lifetime. It also means that 25% of us are permanently suffering from mental health problems. That paints a very different image from the numbers I had heard, not what I envisaged at all. But wait!

One in six people report experiencing a common mental health problem (such as anxiety or depression) in any given week.

What the hell was the first lot referring to then? The second figure of one in six people per week for a "common" problem means the first figure refers to something else, more serious mental illnesses. This also means that I will have one of these "common" problems nine or ten times a year. Not quite the one in four in our lifetime that we first thought, right?

When you look closely, you start to see a very different view. We are a nation of pill poppers and if we are not on statins, we are on antidepressants, sleeping tablets, painkillers, or beta blockers.

Again, in my view, this all stems from the lack of "Happy Class", no "good mental health" class at school, just tutoring on consumption and greed. I believe that the statistics are wrong anyway. It's actually one in one. Everybody goes through personal problems at some point in their life. If you didn't, you would never learn anything and never evolve or grow. Even with the one in four statistic, a quarter of the people I know have never discussed this with me. We live in a culture where we don't talk about it. In reality, if 25% of people a year report it, then the figure is much higher than this. I think the majority of the population feel uncomfortable with this topic and aren't able to share their experiences. Insomnia, high levels of stress, panic attacks, anxiety, phobias, excessive worrying and anger are all mental health issues. Yes, even anger; a person in balance does not let external events control their internal emotional state. Anger is like a hot coal: until you get rid of it, it actually does you, the person carrying it, the most harm, damaging you both mentally and physically. If you express it, that's good. You need to get it out. Like a pressure cooker, you need to release it bit by bit. If you don't, you will blow. However, if you just give it to someone else in rage, then you do them harm too and that just magnifies the problem. If one flame can light a thousand candles, then one fire can burn a thousand bushes. The answer is that we have to start being honest, not covering things up, but instead talking openly about them, and then we will soon realise that we are all the same. We are all broken. None of us are perfect and it's okay not to be okay. Well, actually we are all perfect, but not as in the current view programmed into the masses and portrayed by the media. How can we all learn anything if we don't talk about it? It's like we are stuck in Edwardian times. Don't get me started on that.

"Children should be seen and not heard." What a load of drivel!

Right, I'm back from my tangent now.

"Return of the Mack. Yes, it is..."—Mark Morrison

So the counselling didn't work for me. I wasn't ready to share. I just got angry and then stopped going. When you don't feel good inside, that's what you'll see outside. I imagined what everyone would be thinking, that I was ignorant, lazy, or just simply not a very nice person. Nobody knew that I was ill. I literally couldn't even pick up the phone there for a while. I had very severe anxiety every time it rang. I imagined it being work. My phone used to ring constantly on site. Every time I picked it up, there would be a major problem or at the very least it would be an unpleasant call. In the roles I had done over the years, I had seen people killed or badly injured. These were very high-pressured jobs and hence incredibly stressful. I started out as a site engineer and then moved into management. I worked in many disciplines within the construction industry, each time stepping up to take the most highly paid position I could. I eventually moved into tunnelling, sometimes running several projects simultaneously. At the time I had "a wobble", when all this happened, I was just running one contract in Wales. Everyone I knew in the tunnelling industry who was still able to turn up for work had serious health issues. These were usually stress, anxiety, insomnia, and also heart and nerve problems. It was a male-dominated world, full of macho bravado and big egos. Everyone puffed their chests out and then got angry and shouted a lot. This included me. I would match their frequency. Foul-mouthed rants were the norm. "I'm just going to throw some f**ks into the lads!" I would hear. "It's the only language they understand." It was horrible. Quite often, the people that did really well in the industry had just learned how to deflect blame, directing their problems onto someone else when things went wrong. It was all about covering your arse. There was very little room for error. Sometimes a few millimetres out could mean disaster. Although everyone tried their best, safety was very difficult to manage. This was a massive issue for me. I had many sleepless nights over this. If there was an incident, the buck stopped with me. If one of the lads got hurt, it was on my shoulders. Fortunately, although I had witnessed many bad accidents, nobody under my control ever got badly injured. There's a very important point I would just like to make here. Later in my career, I predominantly did contract work. This meant that I would do very long hours staying away from home for several months at a time. I would live like a monk for long periods, so no partying here then. I could be very disciplined while I was away working, but I was highly stressed and deeply unhappy, with no joy in my life. It simply wasn't possible to work twenty hours a day and then do anything else. However, I would then have some time off, to "recover", and that's when I partied. It was a very unhealthy cycle. My career was basically hell on earth for me and I know this isn't very Buddhist, but I hated it—Ommmmm!

I have to stop and meditate for a minute now. I haven't reached enlightenment yet, and until I do, even just thinking about this time in my life makes me anxious. Although it's very rare that I do now, this still generates lots of negative feelings and emotions. Once you get off this treadmill, you'll never want to get back on. Going backwards isn't an option. So, running alongside my work, my personal life was also a train wreck. All my friends used to think I was mental and I was notorious for my parties when I was back at home. They sometimes went on for days. Well, they always went on for days, if I'm being honest! Note to self—be honest! Now, since I became a Buddhist, the friends that I had left, the ones that were still around after my awakening, that I still had contact with, thought I had gone completely off the rails this time and that I had joined a cult. Fortunately, I had already been shaving my head "Bic bald" for the past twenty years, so I got away with that one. The reality was that after the shift, I had quit my job and cut off almost all my ties to the outside world for a while. I removed myself from my existing social life and slowly started to become aware of my true self and all of the destructive patterns I had created and that I was repeating.

"Know thyself."—Socrates

"To thine own self be true."—Shakespeare

There were two women who stood by me the whole time, which can't have been easy for them. My mum and Stephanie. Thank you. You're okay, I'm okay. I decided that I needed some time to think. I had so many issues and I had so many questions. My life had no meaning. I had lost my way and everything I had done up to this point seemed futile. I had realised that everything was "a Lie". I knew I had to go right back to the beginning and make some fundamental changes. I needed to start rebuilding from the foundations up. To reboot and re-programme.

"If something is broken, in order to fix it, you must first take it apart and look inside." —MM

In order to do this, I needed to be alone and get really quiet. I started to read about meditation and going on retreat.

"To see celestial majesty, you have to retreat from the fire." —MM

"The closer to the light, the brighter you shine." —MM

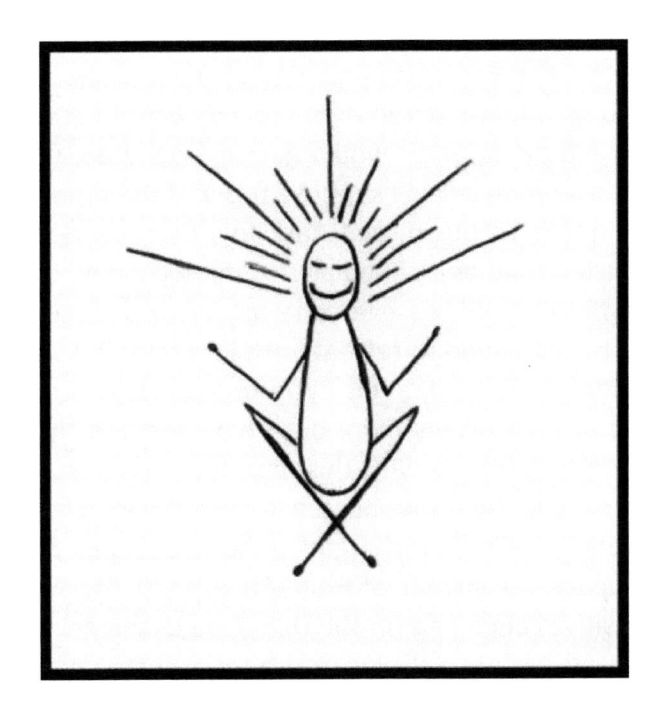

"BEING HAPPY"

BEING HAPPY

I was always a person who needed to spend time on my own. Too much social interaction or company, without some spells of peace and quiet, and I would get very agitated, withdraw, and push everyone away. I suppose this was the time I needed to heal myself. To put myself back together, every time the cracks started to appear. I had always dipped in and out of the social world. I would see everyone for a few days or a week, but then I would need to retreat back into myself. I wanted to be left alone for a while. This cycle repeats to this day. I still need lots of time on my own, but I have learned to see that there is nothing wrong with this, and that it is part of who I am. So, I have learned to embrace it. Except now, when I have some "quiet time", it's recharging my energy levels from, say, +5 back up to +10, instead of from -10 up to -5. Always staying in the positive range and on the right side of things. I love the time I spend both in solitude and also in company, with my friends and the people I love.

There are two ways you can make the people you love in this world happy.

One is to be subservient to others, doing things from motivation born out of obligation, and they are usually things that you don't want to do. You will probably resent this and possibly the person you are doing it for. As a result, you won't be happy and you won't enjoy yourself, nor will the people around you that you do these things for. These actions are not done out of love and this will show. Remember, if you squeeze someone, they can only give out what they have inside.

The other is to start by being honest with yourself and other people. It is to start being selfish. Hold up, did he say selfish? That's right. Now, I don't mean selfish as in saying "Sod off" to everyone else, I mean selfish as in self-love, forgiving and respecting yourself. So not actually being subservient, but following your own path, which will probably still be helping others if it is the right one. Making sure you get plenty of rest and looking after yourself is crucial. Then all you have to do is follow your heart, your dreams, and hence your dharma.

"If you follow your own path, you can't get lost! When you're a pioneer, there is no map."—MM

When you do this, four things will happen.

1. **You will be happy and full of joy.**

2. **The people who truly love you will be happy too** These people will see how happy you are. They will not, like some others, try to control you by pulling at your heart strings. This is basically using emotional blackmail, trying to manipulate you with emotions, to impose their will. Trying to get you to do what they want, out of a sense of honour and duty. Making you feel guilty and using your bad programming against you.

3. **Your flame will shine brightly when you're in a state of joy.** This will spread. You will give this to everyone you meet. Your cup will be overflowing, so you will have lots of free love and energy to give to everyone else, without diminishing your own. You will be like a ray of sunshine, a brilliant star beaming with bliss.

4. **Now, here is the big kicker**—because you're so very happy and following your dharma, you have boundless energy. All your actions are driven out of love instead of obligation, and you feel good. You see, when someone asked you to do something for them that you didn't want to previously, you usually did it but didn't enjoy it. This time you choose to do it willingly and feel empowered. This way, you end up doing it anyway, out of love!

See, the same end result, but different motivations and intention. The same external events, but the thought process to arrive there is different. In this first instance, obligation, in the second instance, love. In this first way, controlled, in the second, empowered with freedom. You can see now that your thoughts about something and your motivation for doing it can change how you feel, even if the outcome is the same. It is your thoughts about an external event that control how you feel, not the external event. So to be truly happy, we have to remove the negative patterns and bad programming we have been given. This can be done through meditation and correct thinking, and then following your heart, your bliss, and your joy. The music inside is your dharma. Dance to your song.

"Unconditional love comes from unconditional thinking."—MM

SANCTUARY OF THE MIND

There's a quiet oasis inside my mind,

There's a peaceful place I can always find.

A parallel place in my control, a balanced pathway for my soul.

Where silence fills my waiting mind, like music fills a song.

With visions painting happiness, in places I belong.

With therapeutic wavelength, and soft empathic style.

This silent curve of every word, that triggers off your smile.

This secret inspiration that whispers words to you.

Invisibly unfolding, its sense of "Déjà Vu".

This pathway to destiny, this stairway that I see.

That winds along beside me, to set my spirit free.

Mystically unfolding, but just within control,

The silent words it's speaking,

are the words straight from my soul.

Their echo that resonates, as inner-visions sway.

Would make me all that I could be,

And more than words could say.

But locked within their meaning,

Is the strength to reach my goal.

As the words of tranquil silence,

Match the silence of my soul.

Within this sanctuary of happiness, I let my soul belong,

Within the sounds it's singing I can live within this song.

Its distant echo's calling, from the other side of me,

Each timeless moment waiting, to set my spirit free.

Creatively, to visualise from the living conscious stream,

Surrendering the daily thoughts, from a distant waking dream.

To travel through each universe beyond each world I go,

To dance on shadowless rainbows

To make the moonbeams glow.

And chase the wind across the sky,

Whilst hidden from its rhyme.

To cast a different shadow, that's gone before it's time.

With magic inner-visions shedding light inside of me.

As time stops in the moment to set my spirit free.

To travel on its pathway to swim within the stream.

Escaping earthly gravity within a parallel dream.

Unlocking new horizons that reach beyond the sky,

Transcending mental boundaries that never question why.

The silence that enfolds me, will make my spirit strong,

As I dance within its music,

I will let my soul belong.

A poem by my friend, D.W. Parry.

<u>Okay, now it's time to get this party started.</u>

<u>Let's talk meditation. Let's do this. Fist pump. Hell yeah!</u>

"If you want a peaceful nation, practice meditation. It all starts with you." —MM

"GOING INTO THE GAP"

4. MEDITATION

Oh, by the way, did I mention I am an Iron Man? Haha!

So, I wanted to learn how to meditate, which is also referred to as "going into the gap" between thoughts. I will try to work my way through this process with a series of questions—this is how I would normally approach it in one of my talks. I hope that one day, at some point in the future, maybe you will be able to come and join me, either in a meditation session or at one of my workshops.

WHY DO WE NEED TO MEDITATE?

Okay, so, why do we need to meditate? If you're already happy and experiencing inner peace on a regular basis, living your life in the moment and spending your days in bliss, then you either already meditate or don't need to. However, if you are like me and the rest of the population on this planet, we get stressed.

There are many other techniques to find inner peace and become fully present and I will mention and discuss some of them later in this chapter. However, in my experience, the most commonly used method around the world, predominantly in the East, with the best chances of success and achieving the desired results, is meditation.

"Stress is mind created. Your stress is your problem!"—MM

"STRESS"

STRESS

"All problems, delusions, and unhappiness are created by the mind. It is not our external circumstances or events that cause these feelings, but our thoughts about them and our reactions to them, that are responsible for our suffering. If we can learn to control our thoughts, we can be permanently happy and live in bliss. This can be achieved through a regular meditation practice."—MM

Stress is when we put a system under strain. It's when we exert forces on it that place it under pressure. If the stress is too great and the system in question was not designed to take those loadings, it will be unable to sustain the situation and the system will break. When we talk about stress, for the purposes of this book, I am going to refer to mental stress. Of course there is emotional stress too, but as you will discover, our feelings and emotions are created by our thoughts. They are a response to how we think about our external environment. Then there is also physical stress.

According to Occupational Health and Safety news and the National Council on Compensation of Insurance, up to 90% of all visits to primary care physicians are for stress-related complaints.

So, up to 90% illness or physical stress is caused by thought too. If you have negative thoughts, they have an adverse effect on your body and physical health. This is a fact. Let's take a quick look at physical stress that is caused by an external force, for example a car crash. If it was your driving that caused the accident, then you probably weren't fully present and paying attention. Your mind was busy thinking about something else at that moment rather than driving the car, or maybe you were driving too fast because you were rushing or because of your emotional state, all caused by an overactive and uncontrolled mind.

If the "accident" was completely out of your control and the other driver was deemed responsible, then the exact same logic applies to their mind. As you will come to see, there are no accidents in this universe, in this perfectly designed system. The true nature of all things is divine. No mistakes.

"In this universal intelligent system, everything is as it should be. Therefore, nothing is as it should be too. So there is nothing to worry about. It's all in divine order."—MM

You see, however you break it down, it always comes back to our mind and our thoughts. Oh, and to boot, if we had a crash but we had inner peace and calm, we would heal a whole lot quicker too. Nearly all "accidents" are caused by one of the parties involved not being fully present, and hence they are avoidable. I know this to be true from my own experiences on site. I have done a number of accident reports and taken many witness statements when someone gets hurt. I have witnessed many serious injuries and also been present in far worse cases.

For those of you that like to push the envelope with the most extreme examples, let's use an earthquake. No, there's not a whole lot you can do about it in that instance. If you crash your car whilst there are tremors coming up from the ground below, then it is not due to a lack of personal presence. I do, however, think that this is an act of nature, Mother Earth letting us know that we are killing the planet and that she is suffering too.

Try this—imagine you are making a cup of tea. You are fully present in the moment and concentrating 100% on the task in hand. You are not in a rush, every action is deliberate and slow, and your mind is only thinking about the tea you are making at that time. Basically, there is nothing else in the world except you and this cup of tea. Oh, and no one else is anywhere near you and there are no trap doors, no earthquakes or rogue derailed trams heading your way. Your environment is safe. You get me. It would be nearly impossible for you to spill this cup of tea, right? This is what Zen Buddhists do when they have a Japanese tea ceremony. It takes a very long time. They become fully present in that moment by going into their actions, into the realm of the five senses. Have you ever been to a Zen Buddhist garden? It's like everything you're seeing is being done in slow motion. It is so beautiful to watch and very peaceful. You see, if you are completely focused on what you are doing and you are competent, you cannot have an accident, unless something beyond your control interjects, like a meteor colliding with our planet, but that's out of your hands so there is no point in worrying about those things that you can't control. Almost every single accident not caused by an external force such as an "act of God" can be avoided, by correct action from the person or persons involved. I digress.

So stress, mental stress, is from an overactive, uncontrolled, and as yet untrained mind. It's like a ship lost at sea with no rudder, being tossed around and battered by a storm. You're at the mercy of every external event, letting them control how you feel, but it is our thoughts about these events, not the external event itself, which control our inner emotional state. Through this analogy, I hope you can now start to see that we are actually the cause of our own suffering and are responsible for it. This cycle will continue until we learn to control our mind, breaking the old patterns and practising correct thought. We can do this in several ways, such as in the discipline of meditation.

Let's say two people are standing at the top of a cliff. One person feels exhilarated, inspired, and alive, surrounded by nature and the incredible views. They are in ecstasy. The other is terrified. He or she is on their knees, clutching at the grass in fear, because they are scared of heights. This fear is mind created. You see, here are two different people, in exactly the same external circumstances and environment, but depending on their thoughts about it, life in that moment is either heaven or hell.

Similarly, imagine that a football team scores a goal. One person is elated and jumps into the air celebrating. The other is sad, heartbroken, and in dismay. Yet again, it is exactly the same sequence of events that occurred for all present, but viewed by different people, with different opinions and thoughts, the experience is completely different. Whether you derive pleasure or suffering from that situation is totally dependent upon what occurs in your mind.

Or finally, a car alarm goes off at work; everyone holds their breath while they wait for the news. They are all very relieved when they find out that it is not their car that has been damaged. Phew. Well, nearly all, apart from some poor soul who is crying in the other corner of the room. These are all ego-based reactions and thoughts. We are also touching on the principle of non-attachment here, but we will not go into this just yet. So I hope from these examples that you get the idea now. You are responsible for your inner emotional state and your happiness, no one else. Blame has no place in a healthy mind. Practice acceptance, forgiveness, non-attachment, and surrendering to the moment. This is the path to enlightenment.

Imagine if we had the power to change and hence control our thoughts. Imagine if we could decide how we were going to feel. Imagine if we could choose to feel good. What a huge effect this would have on our lives and that of the lives of everyone we came into contact with. All our friends, families and even complete strangers would receive it. Going through our day spreading the light, giving peace and love to everyone we meet.

"Thousands of candles can be lit from a single one, and its life will not be shortened. Happiness never decreases by being shared."—Buddha

Well, this is what I am going to show you. You will begin anew. You will start to feel empowered and no longer like a victim.

No longer giving external events and other people the power to control how you feel; you can take charge of your inner world and your emotional state. Let's do this!

"All power is from within and therefore under our control."—Robert Collier

"All that we are is the result of what we have thought."—Buddha

"Whether you think you can or think you can't, either way you are right."—Henry Ford

All three of these previous quotes are tattooed on my body. They are from when I first read the book *The Secret* in 2006. This had a profound effect on me.

"The good news is that the moment you decide that what you know is more important than what you have been taught to believe, you will have shifted gears in your quest for abundance. Success comes from within, not from without."—Ralph Waldo Emerson

A quick tangent here—I often hear the words to the song *Dedication* in my head. It is the old theme tune to *Record Breakers*. It is a fond memory from my childhood. It was sung and played by Roy Castle on his trumpet. What a guy. Except in my version, I substitute the word "meditation" for "dedication". I derive much humour and pleasure from this. I also like to joke that in my classes, "I have been overdoing it, telling everyone not to overdo it, and that I have been getting stressed about meditating." It's always good to add a bit of humour where possible.

"I am depressed. I now regret getting annoyed with myself, about getting frustrated over my excessive worrying, about feeling guilty about becoming angry. I feel ashamed about blaming someone else for my anxiety and letting them disturb my inner peace." Haha! Only you can disturb your inner peace. Can you see how silly this all is now? How all our problems are mind created and come from within? How we manage to tie ourselves up in knots and waste so much energy? How, by using correct thought patterns, all this would go away?

"Frustration is like shouting "Fire!" when you light a match; it makes a problem far bigger than it needs to be."—MM

So, back to stress. Mental stress is our thoughts about an external event. This is the main source of all our problems and has a very negative effect on our mind, body, and emotional state.

Now, I break this stress up into two types.

1. **A present moment reaction to an external event.**

    This can be improved by developing inner peace and introducing a small pause before making any decision.

Once we develop inner peace, it is like a deep lake. External events are just like ripples on the surface of the water and don't disturb our inner emotional state. This analogy is often used by Eckhart Tolle.

For example:

Your car breaks down—get it fixed!

Someone's late for an appointment with you—meditate!

Your friend hasn't rung you—so what!

You have no money—walk in nature!

You have a bill that you can't pay—then don't pay it!

You see, none of these situations require an emotional response, just an action.
It doesn't mean that you have no emotions and it certainly doesn't mean that you don't express them. What it means is that you don't have to have an emotional response to every external event, especially ones about material things that you have no control over. That would just be futile; a complete waste of energy, and it would cause unnecessary anguish. So if you're stuck in traffic, put on your favourite music and celebrate or, like I do, put on your favourite audiobook. I mean, what could be better than listening to an hour of Dr Wayne Dyer, Deepak Chopra, or Eckhart Tolle on a journey in my car just before a meeting? I mean, come on, this is a fantastic

opportunity! In fact, I am pulling out the big guns now—"Rock on Tommy!"
(For the kids at home, this is the catch phrase from *The Cannon and Ball Show*).
I am to cool for school!

Obviously if a family member dies then you will have an emotional response, but this is healthy, part of the grieving process, and an expression of your loss. Although, as Buddhists, we believe that nobody ever really dies! We just return home.

2. **Thoughts about past and future events.**

Don't be fooled here though, these thoughts are still in the present moment!

"Regret is like tying a noose around the neck of the present moment and then pulling the rope tight. It strangles any chance of joy or bliss. Similarly, worry is like holding the present moment to ransom. Refusing to let it go until you get your desired outcome. This will never work; you will be forever a kidnapper, permanently holding the present moment captive. Never being able to enjoy your life. The universe doesn't respond to blackmail, it operates in complete harmony without resistance. It only responds to love."—MM

This second category of stress can be dealt with from a state of inner peace, but also by becoming fully present and developing awareness. Imagine you are on a mountain and at the very top of that mountain is the present moment. When you get there, all your thoughts about the past roll down the left-hand side of the mountain and all your thoughts about the future roll down the right. There is no room on the top of the mountain for anything except your true self in that perfect moment. This is being fully present. The only thoughts that can occur here are about this actual moment, nothing else. To be in the moment, every part of you has to be there. When you are in the now by definition, it is impossible to be stressed. Those thoughts can't exist here or your mind would be out of the now and thinking about past or future events. You learn to let go of all other thoughts, everything. You have to; it is part of this process. Only thinking about the "now"!

The term "mindfulness" is very commonplace these days. Although I didn't really want to go there at first, I do now use it.

I learnt a great lesson here. At first, I just viewed it as a buzzword to sell certain meditation techniques to everyone. Techniques that are actually thousands of years old. Then however, I started to realise that this was a term everyone seemed to be drawn to and that it was actually getting people who previously wouldn't have, to try meditation. There are various types of mindfulness and it can be taught and practiced in different ways. I mainly use Buddhist mindfulness techniques, although I have tried others too. I have come to understand that this did for meditation what MMA did for jiu-jitsu. It got a lot of people to start trying it, taking it more seriously, and then practising it, and hence it has become very popular again, because it is "cool". It's a lot more palatable than "Mahamudra" or "1000 Armed Avalokiteshvara".

So cast your opinions to the side and throw your judgements away. I had to. Mindfulness is spreading the word. It is encouraging lots of people to meditate and thus to experience inner peace, and that has to be a good thing!

So "mindfulness" it is!

Oh yes. Where where we? Thoughts about past or future events.

Most of us at some point have driven to work, right? Have you ever arrived there and then had absolutely no recollection whatsoever of the journey you just took? I have. I used to know someone who boiled the kettle twenty times or more before they finally managed to regain focus, remembering the task in hand and what they were supposed to be doing, making a cup of tea. This was because their mind was so busy, they sometimes couldn't concentrate for longer than a few seconds. They were like a goldfish and their electricity bill was huge! You know who you are. Our minds are so busy thinking about past and future events that often our thoughts are completely out of alignment with the present moment. We literally aren't even "present" most of time. We are just there in body, but not in mind. When we are fully present, our thoughts are aligned with the now and there can be no stress. There is no room. This reminds me of an old children's television programme from when I was much younger, *Play School*. Every day they took you through one of three differently shaped windows and told you a story.

"The present moment has a round door; anything with sides can't get in."—MM

If something has already happened then we cannot change it and feelings like regret and guilt are a complete waste of time and energy. They cause unnecessary suffering and can lead to depression. We need to learn to let go.

"No one ever dies from a snake bite; the venom that continues to pour through your system after the bite is what will destroy you."—Dr Wayne Dyer

It's not the actual event that will get you, but in this instance, the negative thoughts that are left behind, long afterwards.

"The wake can't drive the boat. It's just the trail that's left behind."—Alan Watts

"Your past doesn't define you. It is simply the view on the journey to this moment."—MM

"If you are always looking behind, you will trip up."—MM

"Whatever you focus on, you feed and move towards it."—MM

When you let go of your past, it is like cutting through the ropes that have tethered you to the docks, finally allowing you to set sail. We are all beautiful vessels that were meant to roam free, to journey the seas on a voyage of self-discovery, exploring our full potential. Not like most of us, spending our whole lives moored up in the quays, never knowing what might have been and the splendour that awaits. It's like putting down a big bag of bricks that you have been carrying around with you your whole life. You will feel truly liberated and experience a huge sense of relief and release. You will experience freedom.

"Freedom is just another word for nothing left to lose!"—Janis Joplin

"In order to move forward, you have to let go of the ropes!"—MM

Now, if something hasn't happened yet, then yes, there is obviously still a mental process required, some choices to make, and then of course the appropriate action to take, but that's it. Anxiety, worry, and panic are not "required reading", they are not mandatory; they are all excessive negative thoughts. They are born out of a fear of the unknown, all thoughts about possible future events that are out of your control and that have not actually occurred yet and by all accounts probably won't. As humans, our lives are full of suffering; we spend our time thinking about all of the different futures that could occur, usually all of the things that could potentially go wrong, no matter how unlikely. We are programmed this way. We make a mental list of a hundred negative outcomes and then work our way through them one at a time, imagining, visualising, and hence experiencing all of the attached feelings. In some cases, these can be very unpleasant emotions. In the worst-case scenario, and assuming that a negative outcome ensues, only one of them can actually be brought into fruition and manifest into this realm. Even with an undesirable outcome, the other ninety-nine of them are fiction and a huge drain on our mind and body. These unwanted thoughts can then also stop you from ever making a decision, and indecision can be the biggest thief of all.

"Indecision is the thief of opportunity!"—Jim Rohn

Indecision through overthinking prevents action and produces nothing. You can end up stuck in the docks, never to set sail, and living in fear. You can be completely incapacitated and feel trapped and, consequently, highly stressed.

As we now know, this stress has a very negative impact on our health and also many other aspects of our lives too.

High blood pressure, loss of appetite, hives, lack of sleep, reducing the effectiveness of the immune system, and slowing down any healing processes. Your body's nature is to repair itself and in order for your cells to follow their dharma, to heal and to grow, you must first fulfil yours. With the negative thoughts that we generate, we get in the way of this process.

There are an infinite number of other negative effects of stress on our health.

Inaction through choice is a whole different ball game though. This is often called "the path of least resistance" or "the law of least effort" if you listen to Deepak Chopra.

Right or wrong, a decision followed by the necessary associated action produces a result. There are no failures here, just lessons learnt that then help us to navigate and plot a new course. Even if it's not the result you wanted, you can just accept it and learn a valuable lesson. Gaining more experience each time and then pressing on in a new direction and trying again. Always ensuring that you maintain your momentum and keep moving forward.

"Don't fall down, fall forward. This is still progress!"—MM

"You miss 100% of the shots you don't take!"—Wayne Gretzky

I personally believe that if we remove stress from our mind and then create a non-acidic environment within our bodies, cancer cannot grow, or even continue to exist for long if it is already present. Stress puts strain on the body and hence its cells, causing them to mutate, and then those cells feed on sugar. Refined sugar is cancer's favourite food and best friend, and it's in virtually all processed food. Two people can smoke all their lives, leading an almost identical existence, in the same external environment. Like twins, if you will. One of them then dies of lung cancer at fifty-five and the other manages to live to be one hundred years old. Both smoke. Now, this doesn't mean that cigarettes don't cause cancer, they definitely do, but for some reason smoking kills some people and not others. Why is that? I believe that the key to this enigma is stress. It is the trigger or catalyst for this process, and if you take stress out of the equation, your chances of survival are greatly improved. Your body is a self-healing miracle machine. If nurtured and given a combination of the correct rest and exercise it needs, operating in a mode of low stress and using the correct fuel, it can heal almost anything. Even with just two of these three, a peaceful mind plus one other, the body can experience great healing. Without a peaceful mind, however, the body struggles to repair itself. A very busy uncontrolled mind with the corresponding negative thoughts interrupts the body's nature. It blocks the flow of universal energy and does not allow the cells to function properly and follow their dharma, and hence prevents healing.

So we basically spend all our time worrying and miss the moment. Some of us can spend our lives like this. What a waste, never really living, never being in the now. They say you can't start living until you accept that you're dying. Well, we are all dying. It's only then that we can appreciate every day and start living in the present.

Animals are always fully present. All of nature is fully present. They are fulfilling their true nature, their dharma. Ask an animal what time it is and he will say "It's now, of course." Human beings are the only species to have this absence of presence. The only animals that can ever experience this are usually domestic and if not, they have definitely been in close proximity to or contact with people. You see, just being around someone who isn't present and is highly stressed can have a negative effect on you. Dogs can be depressed if their "owners" are.

Dogs can also live in fear and be highly stressed and anxious if their "owners" are. You get the idea. By the way, nobody can ever really "own" a dog, but they can be their best friend and look after them.

Oh yes, and a note about worry. Do you know what worry is?

I had someone ask me, "If you care about someone, you worry. I can't help it! If I don't worry, doesn't that mean I don't care?"

No. Absolute nonsense!

Compassion and action is the correct path to follow. Compassion is one of the fundamental principles of Buddhism. Compassion is having a deep understanding and empathy for someone who is suffering, born out of love. If you care and have compassion for someone, then by all means, act accordingly, help them in any way you can, assuming that it is wanted. Worry is a whole different matter. It is just negative thoughts about a situation or person, without any action being taken. It may be born from compassion, but it is a destructive force for both parties involved. Act or don't act and then meditate. Worrying doesn't help anyone. It has become part of most people's bad programming. They are hardwired for excessive worrying. Let's be clear: not worrying doesn't mean that you don't care. It means that you can't control the outcome of a situation and you have realised that no course of action available to you will help in any way. It is called acceptance. In this realm, there is an infinite possibility of outcomes that may occur. No amount of worrying will help you control or change this. It will, however, have a negative effect on your health and you will also give this low frequency negative vibration to every around you.

Remember, "The prisons we all live in are constructed by the mind."—MM

"WORRY"

WORRY

My definition of worry!

By the way, a lot of the definitions I use in this book are how I like to explain things, the way that makes the most sense to me, and are not necessarily from a dictionary.

Worry is your negative thought patterns about future events that you cannot control.

It can also be about the consequence of a past event, but that possible outcome is still in the future. If something has already happened then there is nothing to worry about. You may feel guilt, remorse, or regret, because you haven't let go yet, but not worry. Worry is always about what is yet to come. For some reason, we think that it's correct behaviour to worry about other people, to have negative thoughts about them or their potential actions, and then relay this to the parties involved. As if it was a sign of affection. It is not. It can also be used to control or manipulate someone. In seeing how "worried" someone is, how worried "you" have made them, they can pull on your heart strings, using guilt and emotional blackmail to discretely impose their will. Until eventually you decide to avert your course of action altogether to reduce their stress. This is no life. This is not living. This is not following your dharma. It is being manipulated and succumbing to the will of others.

Now, let's be clear, it is not your actions that are the cause of the worry. As we have said, worry is negative thought patterns that are mind created and that come from within. It is the other person's thoughts about these external events and that is their problem to address.

"Be independent of the good opinion of other people." — Abraham Maslow

Now, when someone worries about you and then tells you about it, this can create anxiety. Through relaying this message and by spreading the fear, they are also sowing the seeds of doubt in your mind, and you can end up averting your course of action yet again. Not because you don't want them to suffer, but this time because you now have fears of your own, were before there were none. This has now affected your confidence and you decide against doing something that you felt inspired about, that you love to do, and hence not fulfilling your dharma, because you are fearful.

For example, I ride my push bike on a regular basis, whenever I can. I absolutely love it, going down hills fast and feeling the wind in my face (not in my hair though because I'm bald). In this moment, I am in bliss. I am fully present. I am very confident on my bike, very alert and assertive, and I react quickly. I feel in complete control and have command of my bike.

The only time I ever had an incident was after I had a ten-minute lecture about all the things that could possibly go wrong, but worse still, not stopping there, the consequences of all the "accidents" I could have, in gory detail. Remember, there are no "accidents".

I am talking severe brain damage, the loss of limbs and paralysis here. So this person managed to project their fears onto me and hence instil their negative thought patterns into my mind. The universe is just a great big cosmic mirror, so it was because they were scared of riding a bike themselves. It is a wonder that they ever manage to leave the house. This was not done because they cared; they were off-loading their own low frequencies onto me. If they cared, they would have kept their mouth closed and their fears to themselves. I let an external source instigate a desired emotional response. I gave someone else control over my inner world. I let them decide how I should feel. A lesson learnt!

So after this lecture, I went out riding on my bike as normal, but I had let fear and doubt creep into my head. Each time I pulled up to an intersection on the road, I was thinking of everything that had been said earlier, about everything that could go wrong, carnage and destruction. My confidence had gone and I definitely wasn't focused on what I was doing and in the moment. I wasn't fully present. My mind was distracted by a sense of doom and dread. Then a car came flying out of a junction, but my decision-making processes and reaction times were hampered. They were much slower than usual, because I wasn't paying attention. Where I was normally assertive, I hesitated. We collided, but I didn't get seriously hurt. I just had cuts and bruises, but it was still a very close call. The next time around, I refused to listen to this negative energy. I requested that they stop, but they refused. Like I said, it is offloading their fears onto others. Trying to get people to match their frequency.

"I have got to tell you. It's only because I care. I can't help it!" and therein lies the rub. "I can't help it." They can't control their mind; it's the result of bad programming, folks.

I blocked it out and this was the last time I can recall raising my voice in anger. I have probably only done this twice in the last five years. It makes me very sad when I lose my cool and resort to this. I need to meditate more! Sometimes, in the past, it has been completely my fault, of course. You see, I have made a lot of mistakes in my life and I'm not perfect and I will continue to do so. I am just trying to be better than I was yesterday. For the person who gave me the lecture on doom and carnage, you can take your worries and gently place them where the sun doesn't shine. Sorry, just having a bit of fun. Thankfully, my confidence returned on my next ride out and again, I now love very single minute on my bike. It's one of my favourite things.

So let's just flip the coin for a moment now. What if you are the person doing the worrying? If you worry about someone else you have some work to do, correcting your thoughts. The correct process is compassion, action, and then acceptance. Sometimes people aren't actually even worried, they just know it is socially acceptable to be seen to say they are, but if you are genuinely worried then certainly don't spread the fear. You could then end up being the cause of the very accident that is the source of your worry. A self-fulfilling prophecy, if you will. It is time for you to meditate.

Besides, I no longer fear death. I am always ready to meet my maker, I tell everyone this, and going fast on my bike would be a good way to go. Being in a state of bliss, doing what I love. Not many people are that lucky.

I don't want to be one hundred years old and die of an illness, because I didn't do any of the things I loved and played it safe, living in fear. Sod that. That's not living. That's no life. Now, if you make it to that age and you've truly lived, I take my hat off to you. You are blessed.

"You need to embrace the unknown until it becomes known." —MM

"You need to throw yourself into the realm of "infinite possibility" and practice "the wisdom of uncertainty.""— Deepak Chopra.

Time is also a big cause of stress. Imagine doing any activity. Now try and do it in half the time. As soon as we put time constraints on a set of activities, that are shorter than the time it takes to actually do them, the whole process loses its enjoyment and becomes stressful. We start to rush around, constantly thinking about the next job on the list, and hence we are distracted and certainly not fully present. The trick is to say, "No. I'm sorry, I can't do the activities that you are asking me to in the time allocated." Trying to do ten things in the time that it should take to do seven is bad practice. You will miss the moment and won't enjoy any of them. Instead, do less. Do six things in the time it takes to do seven and enjoy them all. Have a chat and a cup of tea. Take "your time".

The crazy thing is that a lot of the issues we have with time management are of our own creation. We impose unrealistic time constraints on our "to-do" list and then go about our business. We set ourselves an impossible schedule to achieve and then spend our day running around under pressure. None of our jobs get done any quicker and we don't get any more done. In fact, usually, quite to the contrary, we make mistakes; we are clumsy and sometimes have accidents. So all this stress is self-imposed by people thinking they need to do more, more, and more. They are constantly racing with themselves and against the clock, trying to beat time. There is one thing I know for sure: you will never beat time, at least not in this sense, anyway.

"Do less, accomplish more. This is the law of least effort."— Deepak Chopra

WHAT IS MEDITATION?

Meditation is a set of simple instructions and techniques to enable us to learn how to train the mind and control our thoughts, enabling us to remain calm and focused. Over time and with a regular practice, these techniques then help us to develop inner peace. Then bliss and joy will spontaneously evolve, as this is our natural state and comes from within. Some of the other benefits include relaxation, deep rest, and reduced stress levels.

It is learning how to go into the gap between thoughts.
It is learning how to go into the silence.
It is learning how to become still.

In life, it can feel like we are constantly meeting resistance, pushing in every direction, spending lots of energy and getting nowhere. You are swimming upstream, going against the flow of universal energy and natural law. Stop pushing so hard and slow down. Relax! We have been looking in all the wrong places. If you are looking for happiness outside you will never find it. The doors open inwards.

Remember, "You can go within, or go without."—MM (Paraphrased from Ralph Waldo Emerson)

"Infinite patience produces immediate results." — *A Course in Miracles*

MEDITATION JOURNEY

Within the dreams of everyone, if they can unlock their mind.

Like magic inner visions just waiting to unwind.

They'll take you on a journey, to a brightly shining star.

They'll show you the key to unlock your soul,

And show you who you are.

On a voyage of discovery, to see all you could see.

To a place that feels like freedom, to be who you could be.

Outside of your experience, but still in your control.

Invisible connections guide, the journey of your soul.

Each new place that you journey, and each new place you view.

Each day that you discover, another piece of you.

On a voyage of discovery you'll travel near and far.

To know just who you're really not, to be just who you are.

Like a sunrise, softly dawning in the corner of your mind.

Like a dream you once remembered, let your journey now unwind.

To a place you've never been before, that's just beyond your view.

A place that's waiting patiently, somewhere inside of you.

As soft as the breeze that travels, though invisible to you.

The road that is your journey, unwind with "Déjà Vu"

When your soul is softly shining, like a distant pulsing star.

Your truth is softly dawning,

And you can, be who you are.

It's the journey you travel as thoughts unwind.

To the places of dreams in a conscious mind.

To the melting pot of reason, your thoughts may softly go.

It's the therapy not the reason of a place you don't yet know.

It's another piece of the jigsaw, coming softly into view.

Another journey that may unlock, another part of you.

In the distance, not yet travelled, is an answer you may find.

But only completing the journey, can place these thoughts in your mind.

It's the people and places on the journeys you meet,

It's the jigsaw that helps make your life complete.

'Cos your life is a circle, a slow spinning wheel,

When you've lived your life well you'll know when it's real.

Follow your soul's intuition now your journey has begun.

It's the only one who can lead you to, the hero you may become.

It's the journey we travel unbroken, beyond, around, and within.

If we listen to our soul when it's talking, these words let our journey begin.

To each unknown destination the gentle roads unwind.

With invisible direction, that only your soul can find.

Follow each road on your journey, as it unwinds the time that you live.

Cherish the things that it brings you, like the gifts that are yours to give.

On the road uphill we travel still, on the road we first begun.

But it's the way we travel our journey,

That defines who we become.

A poem by my friend, D.W. Parry.

WHAT ARE THE DIFFERENT TYPES OF MEDITATION?

Even just within Buddhism there are lots of different traditions and many various types of meditation. I am part of the New Kadampa Tradition. This is Mahayana Buddhism.
I am not going to get into this too much now, so here is just a brief explanation of these terms.

"Kadampa Buddhism is a Mahayana Buddhist school founded by the great Indian Buddhist Master Atisha (AD 982-1054).
In the word, 'Kadampa', 'Ka' refers to Buddha's teachings, and 'dam' to Atisha's special Lamrim instructions. Kadampas, then, are practitioners who regard Buddha's teachings as personal instructions and put them into practice by following the instructions of Lamrim.
By integrating their understanding of all Buddha's teachings into their practice of Lamrim, and by integrating their experience of Lamrim into their everyday lives, Kadampas use Buddha's teachings as practical methods for transforming daily activities into the path to enlightenment."— Kadampa.org

Mahayana Buddhism is one of the two major traditions of Buddhism, now practiced especially in China, Tibet, Japan, and Korea. The tradition emerged around the first century AD and is typically concerned with personal spiritual practice and the ideal of the bodhisattva. The word Mahayana is Sanskrit and translated into English means "great vehicle".

Here are just a few sample types of meditation, not just the Buddhist ones. Nearly all are beneficial in some respect and I don't negate any of them.

- Guided meditations, often with music, for relaxation and sleep (more commonly used in the Western world)
- Chanting (meditation using a mantra and maybe some mala beads)
- Prostrations (repeated outward extensions of your body, usually lying face down on the floor)
- Transcendental meditation or TM (used all over the world—which I also practice daily)
- An old Irish Catholic priest using his rosary beads and praying (in effect, chanting and meditating)
- Affirmations (positive statements repeated verbally; "I am love", etc.)
- Focusing on nature—using a flower, for example. Trying to see it with your mind and exploring the object through the realm of the five senses, without labelling it. As if you had just experienced it for the very first time.
- Using the vocalisation of different sounds to match certain frequencies and then resonate with specific parts of the skull, causing them to vibrate. In this instance, to decalcify the pineal gland and re-open the third eye! Yes, folks, really! I have done this! I'm not making this stuff up. Let's do this! Hell yeah! Let's decalcify!

The pineal gland is a very small organ in the centre of the brain. It is also known as the "third eye". It is a small endocrine gland and it produces melatonin. This is a hormone that affects our sleep patterns. It is thought to be the place where all our thoughts are created and come from.

"The principal seat of the soul!" as Descartes called it.

So, you can meditate just about anywhere, but it is good practice to prepare a special space, removing all the audible, visual and mental distractions if possible. I've had a dedicated meditation room with a shrine for several years now. Nothing goes into that room that is not in some way spiritual or related to meditation. Obviously, we don't all have a spare room to do this, but even just a quiet corner of a chosen room will do, somewhere you can prepare for your practice, somewhere that you can have some peace. In theory, if we were all enlightened, we could just sit down and meditate in the middle of a very busy and noisy motorway, not getting run over in the process obviously, although we would heal quicker…just kidding! However, until such time, it is best to give ourselves a fighting chance, and to remove all possible interruptions, interferences, and distractions. For meditation to be effective, it needs to be daily practice, gaining momentum and then developing inner peace as we are "Moving Forward", the title of my second book. Your phone must be switched off when you are doing this! "OFF!" I hear you say. Yes, off. "OMG! I can't do that! What if something terrible happened in those twenty minutes? What if someone had a crash or got ill and they couldn't get hold of me?" Please! Really? What about when you're in the shower or asleep? You're just addicted to technology, and specifically your phone. You're jacked up on a constant influx of emails, texts, and social media. We have become addicted to this constant stream of information. Some people almost have a panic attack when you even suggest having no television for an evening! I digress again!

"We need to disconnect from technology to reconnect with spirit."—MM

It's not forever; it's just for a little while. It's really not that big of an ask. You will live. Just try it once and then see how you feel. Until you can do this, until you can take this small step, you won't know peace. It's your choice. What have you got to lose? So turn your phone off when you meditate, try to only check your phone on your lunch break or at set times, rather than reacting to it constantly every time it beeps, and try to watch as little television as possible. There is a whole new world outside and inside, just waiting to be explored.

Meditation is like medicine. We can read about it in books and study it, but this will not make us better. The knowledge alone will have no effect. We must drink the medicine to heal ourselves. Just as with this analogy, we need to have a regular daily meditation practice to experience the results.

"Ten minutes in the bank, all day at the market." —Maharishi Mahesh Yogi, when referring to the benefits of regular transcendental meditation.

This is when we visit pure consciousness every single day, when we go into the gap and then take this serenity out of the meditation with us, and then spend it as we go around, giving it to everyone we meet. In exactly the same way, a Buddhist develops inner peace and then moves through life with compassion, giving peace and love to all sentient beings.

Whilst teaching the most common excuse I have heard from people, those who are not yet managing to make the necessary space in their lives to meditate and become still, is "I haven't got time!" Well, this simply doesn't wash. Firstly, as I will explain, nobody has time, we have energy, and secondly, we all choose how we spend that energy. We make a list and then prioritise what is important to us and distribute our energy accordingly. If we don't have "time", it is simply deemed as low priority, not important enough, not high enough on the list for us to allocate our energy to it. That is the honest answer. Yes, sometimes there are things on the list that we don't even actually want to do, that we feel we must, born out of obligation or a sense of duty, but this again is still a choice.

"Nobody has time. You have energy." —MM

Time is a unit of measurement and that's it. It does obviously have practical uses, but that is all. Eckhart Tolle calls this "Clock Time". Imagine if I asked you for a favour.

"Can you give me a hand, John? I need some help."

"No. Sorry, mate. I haven't got enough centimetres."

Sounds silly, doesn't it? You only ever have the present moment, this perfect rolling perpetual now. If I asked you for a piece of yesterday, you couldn't give it to me. If I asked you for a slice of tomorrow, the same applies. You see, none of us have time; it's not real, it's a concept. All we ever have is the present moment. You might think, but tomorrow's not now? Ah well, tomorrow hasn't manifested yet and so it's not happened, but when it does arrive it will be now again. It's always now. Has there ever been a point in your life when if asked what time it was, the answer was not now? Time is simply a system which man has invented to measure, structure, and manage the cyclical movement of life and the flow of universal energy. The good news is that what we do have at our disposal is this energy, and we can decide how we use it. It's a choice. If we are inspired, following our dharma, allowing the energy of the universe to flow through us and living in bliss, we will have a lot of it. If, on the other hand, we are unhappy and trying to fit into the system, believing "The Lie", we will have very little energy and maybe none to spare. Once we understand and learn about the true nature of things, a more honest answer to the previous question might be something like this.

"No. Sorry, mate. I only have a certain amount of energy today and I choose to spend it watching football. You're not on the list."

I will leave the topic of time for now as I don't want to open up this can of worms fully just yet. I could quite happily write an entire book on this one subject. When we start to break it down and look at it more closely with our eyes wide open, it is a revelation.

"If you were on a train travelling overnight and you needed to sleep, would you find somewhere to rest? Yes! If you needed the toilet, would you find a bathroom? Yes! Why can you not find a chair?"—Maharishi Mahesh Yogi.

"Have you got time to eat? Have you got time to breath? That's how important meditation is."—Geshe Kelsang Gyatso

There are no excuses. It is a choice. Meditation is critical to the development of your inner peace and hence, the evolution of mankind. It is part of the answer, raising global awareness and elevating the consciousness of all sentient beings on earth. This includes you.

"If you want to join the party, if you want to be party-pants, you have to be a participant."—MM

DO I NEED TO BE A BUDDHIST TO MEDITATE?

Yes, absolutely, you need to be a Buddhist to meditate.
I am just messing with you. Of course not. But I actually get asked this regularly.
I am very clear at the start of all my workshops now.
I teach meditation.

Buddhism is a separate entity and a personal choice. I found that if Buddhism isn't part of the initial equation, people are much keener to come down and see what all the "quiet" is about. (Chuckle!)
I think uninformed people see Buddhism as some kind of cult, that they eat people's babies or something! For me, Buddhism came naturally and was part of my journey. It went hand in hand with learning meditation and it was on the same path. At the end of the day though, it is up to you. I am, however, heavily influenced by Geshe Kelsang Ghyatso's Buddhist texts and teachings, which would be clear to you if you met me, but that is not my purpose. My purpose is to give everyone the simple skills and techniques needed to reduce stress and alleviate suffering. It is not for the chosen few to reach enlightenment while the rest are living in discomfort, but for everyone to be able to find some inner peace through meditation.

Remember, "Meditation is for everyone!"—MM

MANJUSHRI AND RETREATS

This does now seem like a good time to tell you a little bit more about my journey into Buddhism. My adventure started when I was driving in a car to the Lake District. Like I said, I had a spiritual awakening and was starting to go through the shift. I was looking for answers and knew that I needed to find a better way to switch off my mind. I was looking for peace and definitely no more drama, trying to put some happiness and joy back into my life. I was highly stressed and close to, if not past, breaking point. I wasn't well, suffering from anxiety, panic attacks, and insomnia due to hellish nightmares. A few days prior to this trip, I had been reading about meditation and was fascinated by it, but decided I would need some proper instruction to get started. To temporarily find relief, I went to the lakes for the day, for a ride out and maybe to have a walk in the countryside. By pure chance, and there are no coincidences remember, just synchronicity and alignment, I saw as sign for Manjushri. This was a Buddhist centre with a huge gold temple that you could see from miles away. It was in Ulverston and I had heard about it previously. Perfect. So off I popped to have a look. I knew as soon as I arrived that this was somewhere very special. I could feel the energy, like a wave of peace passing over me. Yes, palpable positive energy, peace and love. Little did I know that this was the mother centre, the headquarters for the New Kadampa tradition.
It is also the centre for Tharpa publications, where all Geshe Kelsang Gyatso's books are printed, he is the founder of this tradition in the UK. This is where the main art studios are located and they make their world famous statues. I visited the temple first, which took my breath away, and then I

walked around the old priory. This building has a long history and has always being a sanctuary for the sick, a place of healing. Then I continued exploring, walking through the woodland, which is where I want my ashes to be spread when the time comes, and then down to the beach. I felt fantastic, alive and excited, better than I had done in a very long time. This was a Wednesday, I think, and could you believe it? There was a five-day retreat starting that Friday! Well, I read all the information and then wanted to think about it for a while and mull it over, but with a bit of friendly persuasion from Stephanie, I booked it there and then. What had I done? I hadn't really thought this through. I liked to think about everything thoroughly first, over and over. I remember a time in my life when I was younger, when if I had an idea and felt inspired, I just did it, following my heart and what felt good. I didn't talk myself out of doing everything by overthinking it. So, to the particulars of my stay. Where would I sleep? I had a bad neck. I would need my special pillow! I can't sleep without a constant supply of fresh air and it needs to be a very cool room. What if I forgot my sleeping tablets? Even with them I averaged two to four hours of sleep a night maximum and I would wake everyone up with my insomnia or need a wee. I always had a thing about not waking someone up when they were asleep, not disturbing them from their peaceful state. If the occasion arose and I needed a wee, would I just hold it in? What if I got hungry in the night? I needed food constantly. I would eat enough for four people back then, but I was three stone heavier and lifted weights five times a week. I have OCD and I am unable to share my space with other people. I was terrified of being in a dorm. I also had a bad back. I was overthinking everything. Doubt was coming on fast, like water into a sinking ship, but it was too late! I had paid in full on the spot. Damn Stephanie, I would think. Now, instead, it's a great big thank you. It turned out to be the best thing I ever did. See, with perspective, things in our life that may seem terrible at the time can turn out to be a blessing and part of our spiritual path, aiding personal development and helping us to grow. Sometimes, looking back, these are the best things that ever happen to us. Follow your bliss and your heart, not your head and your bank balance. The best decisions are made when you go quiet inside and listen to how you feel, and then you're not over-analysing everything. You're not looking at all the terrible things that could happen, all the possible negative outcomes, and hence not being controlled, debilitated, and paralysed by fear. Often, with too much analysis, the result is that you end up doing nothing. Without the loving push I received that day, I wouldn't have gone on my first retreat and I probably wouldn't have learned how to meditate. I wouldn't have written this book, and I may not still be here now to tell my tale. This decision probably saved my life and my sanity.

As discussed earlier, you now know that all of us suffer from common mental health issues at various points throughout our life. We also know that very few people are talking about it. It doesn't mean we are all schizophrenics, but I suppose some of us are. Well, I am, and so am I! It means that at some point most people have "a bit of a wobble". We are all human and so all feel the negative emotional effects of a relationship breakup, a divorce, or a bereavement. These can then develop into insomnia, anxiety, or depression, for example. Depression is when your subconscious mind forces your body to take deep rest.

In my case, it was severe insomnia. I still suffer from it today, although it's much less troubling now, and definitely not as extreme as it was before I went through the shift. I'd had it for years. I took a lot of pills. I went "From Pills to Peace".

Ta-da! Thank you, ladies and gentlemen, we will be here all night. Boom! Elvis has left the building. I was deciding when to officially drop that bomb from the title! Hell yeah! Fist pump! I feel like I have just climbed Mount Everest. Jacked up like a small child on a glass of full-fat Coca Cola, or me on a medium-strength cup of filter coffee. I will explain later why I normally drink "diet coffee". Yes, seriously, that pumped! Sorry, I'm off on a tangent again.

So, try having one or two hours sleep per night for thirty years and see how you fare. Insomnia is brutal. It can break even the toughest people, and I mean mentally not physically strong here. I've seen big tough guys brought to their knees, crying because they become desperate. The symptoms of insomnia affect your thoughts and mind, your outlook on every situation. Little problems become huge dilemmas. It's like time. You can never beat it. You will never win this battle. In its advanced stages, some of the symptoms include depression, paranoia, and hallucinations. At first, I just tried to stay up. This went on for years, but then I had many physical health issues which included a stroke in my late twenties. I was paralysed down one side of my body and it took me months to gradually regain my health. Fortunately, I made a good recovery, but it was very scary. I thought this might be it. I could be stuck this way, I may never get better. It was the not knowing that was terrifying. I once went seven days straight with no sleep. Not good at all. I went over to the dark side. I was seriously messed up. We will leave it there.

Oh yes. To my point.

So I went on a retreat. It was in at the deep end; I was very anxious and well outside of my comfort zone. My anxiety levels were far higher than normal anyway, because I wasn't well. I had never done anything like this before and I was going on my own, on a bunk bed, in a dorm.

To retreat is to step back, to remove yourself from your normal daily routine and environment. This element is crucial. Also to re-treat yourself, to make time for you and to nourish your soul. You gain some well-needed perspective on retreat. You take a proper look at yourself, how you are doing, how you are feeling, and where you are heading. A full life review and introspective mental health check, something that you definitely won't get chance to do at home.

Remember, "To see celestial majesty, you have to retreat from the fire."—MM

If you ever get the chance to go on any kind of retreat, take it. I'm not just referring to Buddhist meditation retreats; I mean any retreat that tickles your fancy. When the opportunity comes your way, do it. Grab it with both hands. You owe it to yourself. Yoga, plant medicine, Ayurveda, transcendental meditation, they all rock!

Remarkable things can happen on retreat.

Here are two key elements that you can do to facilitate a successful retreat.

1. You can remove yourself from your daily routine, people and things. Even if you make time for yourself in your home environment, your mind will be distracted by the details of your life. You will still look at the carpet that really needs cleaning, still look at the bill that needs paying, and there could be a knock at the door or an unwanted phone call at any time. You can't see the wood for the trees. No, no, no. Get out of there and disconnect from everything, even if it's just for a little while.

"In the East they contemplate the forest; in the West we count the trees!"—Dr Wayne Dyer

2. You can unplug. Right, now this means no phone calls, no texts, no emails, no internet, and no television. No exception. That's right; I said no phone and no TV. You will survive, I promise. You have to turn everything off. Prepare everything well before you go. Let everyone who needs to; know that you won't be contactable for a few days. The same applies for work. Sod work. You have to disconnect people. You will always have a to-do list. It will still be there when you get back. It's up to you. How badly do you want change? You need to make the time to reflect and do some inner work, some "soul searching". Yes, if your long-lost aunty has just hours to live, then you have a pass, but to be honest, in this instance, don't go. It's not

your time. Go on the next one when all your relatives have a least a few weeks left and you can turn your phone off.

When I first went on retreat, I just wanted to leave after the first night. I felt so out of my comfort zone with all these "hippies". I felt stupid and became very self-analytical and self-conscious. Everything went quiet; there were no distractions and I didn't like it. If I had gone home that first night, I wouldn't have experienced peace and would not be writing this book right now. Who knows where I would have ended up? I decided to persist with it for one more night. I am so glad I stayed. You see, I thought the problem was my car, my job, and other people. With all those things removed and everyone I was surrounded by being so peaceful, I had contrast, I had perspective, and consequently, for the first time I realised something. I had an "epiphany", I absolutely love this word. It was me. I was the cause of all my suffering. I was the problem. My ego, my thoughts, and my bad programming were the culprits. It was emotional as you can imagine. You see, there is nowhere to hide on retreat, no shopping, no noise, no computers, no technology, and basically no other distractions.

Remember, "All of humanity's problems stem from man's inability to sit quietly in a room alone."—Blaise Pascal

I had to go within and take a good look at myself and I didn't like what I saw, lots of macho nonsense and foolish pride. I used to say that my ego was so big it couldn't get through the door. It couldn't fit in a room with other people with big egos. I knew right then that it was time for change and in order to move forward, I needed to do some major re-programming.

Ironically, one of the highlights of my trip ended up being meeting all the people in the dorm. I started to engage with them and had lots of questions. Lots and lots of questions! They were very patient with me. Monetary wealth meant nothing in this space. There was a doctor, a scientist, a window cleaner, a writer, a builder, and the unemployed.
It just didn't matter. I loved it.

On my way home from that retreat, I experienced inner peace for the first time in my life, ever! I was in bliss for the entire journey home. Driving in silence, in ecstasy, experiencing love and joy all the way to Bolton. It was perfect and very profound. Curiously, another place I have since felt like this was when I hired a narrow boat for three days. I was in nirvana, totally unplugged from the rest of world. I highly recommend this to everyone.

"No Jacket Required!"—an album by Phil Collins

I know this is probably not quite what he meant by the title of this album, but it seems very apt here. You see, I had discovered that I already had everything I needed. I didn't require anything else externally. I just needed to be shown the way back to the light. To reconnect with my true self. It was just locked away deep inside, covered with layer upon layer of bad programming. Masked by lots of lies that I had been told and that I had also told myself to try to fit in and conform. All the answers were there all along. I was a perfect creation of divine intelligence. I was complete and whole. It had been so long since I could recall feeling like this; I felt great, but not like I could remember it, not like it had been before. This was different. It was like I was experiencing it for the very first time, a new level of feeling good. This was in fact joy. I was starting to develop deep inner peace and was in a state of bliss. Heaven on earth, if you will.

THE ANSWER

A POEM BY MIDNIGHT MCBRIDE

The answers you were looking for, were here all along

Inside your heart, in the form of a song

The lyrics are heavenly, about peace and love

The rhythm divine and sent from above

No war, no conflict, no hunger, just peace

This is the way, how all suffering will cease

You see, love is the answer, to every question they pose

It was there all along, right in front of your nose

You need to have courage, to dance to the beat

To laugh and spread joy, moving your feet

You see actions and words, what you do every day

The message you send, and the music you play

It's this that will decide the fate of man

So you must act now and do all that you can

What you do here, you give out to all

This is the time, and it is your call

So now you have the answer, what will you do?

It's time to decide, it's all up to you

You see the treasure inside, from God whence it came

So it's your turn now, you must do the same

Go into the world, and spread the word

It's your time to shine, and you must be heard

Like a radiant star, shone into the night

Changing the world, with your beam so bright

The light from within, is the answer we needed

Now you have shown it, let's hope it's heeded

If you can live in harmony, without any drama

Then my friend, you have followed your dharma

"Don't die with your music still in you!" —Dr Wayne Dyer

After just five days of disconnecting from the outside world, from my current life, I had changed forever. I had seen the light within and I also had my first experience of "satori". This is a sudden, inexpressible feeling of inner understanding. It is seeing into one's true nature, a brief glimpse of oneness, emptiness, or enlightenment. Even though it can last for just a moment, it is a game changer. It is a very profound experience. I had realised that we were all one, all connected and part of an intelligent system, with universal energy flowing through us, if we choose to let it in.

"If you let it, the universe can deliver at the speed of light!"— MM

It was going to be the start of a long process for me, but I had direction now and I had also found something that felt right. I knew this was definitely good for me. I remember being sat in the temple for the first time at night doing sadhana in puja. Sadhana is a practice similar to hymns or prayers and puja is like a mass, if you are a Christian. They are not exactly the same but for our purposes here, I think this comparison will do. Whilst in the temple, all I could see was gold. Everywhere I looked the colours were so vivid. There was gold on the robes of all the Kelsangs, gold on all the different statues, and gold trim all around the temple itself. It was so soothing, peaceful, and beautiful. I can still close my eyes and go there now, visualising the event in great detail. It was a very spiritual experience for me.

Anyway, from this point forward I was a regular visitor at Manjushri. For the next few years, I went on courses and retreats there as often as I could, approximately every four to six weeks. Sometimes, just a quick visit for two days, but usually for longer, five to seven days at a time. Everyone from home thought I had gone completely crazy this time and "lost the plot", but I was used to that by now. I was starting to feel really good about myself. I was starting to heal from within and put myself back together again. That was far more important than what anyone else thought about me now. I won't list everything I have done in this vein, and I am not trying to impress anyone, and besides:

"What you think of me is none of my business."—Dr Wayne Dyer

I am simply trying to give you a rough outline of my journey and what was involved. I have done well in excess of thirty courses and retreats at Manjushri over the last five years. Here are just a few:

> How to understand the mind
> The 35 confession Buddhas
> Kadam lamrim
> Refuge retreat
> Amitayus
> The Oral teachings of Mahamudra
> Mindfulness
> The bodhisattva's way of life

I now practice transcendental meditation daily too!

"This is easy, yes? This is how we meditate!" —Lewis Walch, my TM teacher

I have spent about four months in total on retreat over the last few years. Meditating for up to eight hours a day, sometimes in silence for the duration of the retreat. I have also spent a week meditating on the twenty-one "Lamrim" at Manjushri. This means the "quick path" to enlightenment. I have been lucky enough to do this on more than one occasion and have also been very fortunate to receive many empowerments over this period. If you are a Christian, these are akin to special blessings. Along my journey I have made many new friends, including some of the people who work and live there within the Buddhist community. These include nuns and monks who are resident at Manjushri. I would just like to say a special thank you to Kelsang Chosang. She has always been a good friend to both me and Stephanie and she has been my spiritual guide and a source of inspiration through some difficult times. She has always given me just the right advice, just when I needed to hear it.

Thank you, Kelsang Chosang.

"The frequency you display attracts the people in your day!"— MM

If you get the chance and a window should appear in your busy schedule, get in the car and head to Manjushri in Ulverston for the day. You won't be disappointed and you will love the carrot cake. Since then, I have tried many different types of retreat, not just Buddhist ones. As yet, there have been no disappointments. They have all been incredible.

"When your response to every situation is love, you have become the light!" —MM

"BUDDHISM"

BUDDHISM

It took me a whole year after my first retreat before I could say this out loud.

"I am a Buddhist."

It was a big hurdle for me to get over. I have now learned not to give a monkeys about what other people think about my actions. Obviously I try to act without knowingly causing others any harm or suffering in the process. It is truly liberating to be yourself and it ignites a whole new sense of freedom. I have broken and cast off the self-imposed shackles from my mind. I am free! We are all actually free; we just haven't figured it out yet!

The things that attracted me to Buddhism were:

- It is not a religion; it is a school of thought, a system, all based on the simple techniques and the practice of meditation. So because it isn't one, all other religions are welcome. For example, Sikhs, Hindus, Christians, and Muslims all regularly frequent the temple I go to. If a person is to think that their religion is the right way and everyone else's is wrong, how can we have unity? The only way is the total inclusion and the acceptance of all humanity. Respecting everyone's right to have their own views.

"You can't have world peace if everyone's not invited!"—MM

- You're not going to hell if you have a glass of wine; they just give you guidelines. So you're not being judged and just simply try to do your best.
- They don't kill each other or any other living things for that matter. They have respect and reverence for all living things. However small, they are cherished. Even flies. All life is precious.
- They treat men and women as equals. In fact, most of the senior positions at Manjushri and in the New Kadampa Tradition (NKT) seem to be held by women and not men. Gen-La Kelsang Dekyong, a woman, is the current General Spiritual Director of the NKT and resident teacher at Manjushri. There are many female kelsangs and kadams. A kelsang is someone who has been ordained (nuns and monks) and a kadam is a lay teacher.
- It doesn't matter what sexuality or race you are. They practice non-judgement. All are welcome.
- They invite questions, debate and encourage you to try out and test the techniques of meditation. You don't need to have faith.
- And, wait for it…they like cake! Boom! I'm sold!

I wanted to become ordained at one point and lead the life of a monk. However, I didn't discuss it with anyone or say it out loud until I had given it some serious consideration first. I don't think that is a decision anyone should make lightly. It's a big one. I decided not to go down that route in the end. After lots of contemplation, I concluded that it was not the right path for me at that time. Only one person knows exactly why, but I wasn't ready to commit to all the vows at this stage. I may end up there again one day. Who knows? Maybe now however, after writing this book, with a few profanities thrown in, they may not take me.

You see, for me to be part of any group or perhaps a religion, it has to make sense. I was raised as a Catholic. I was always surprised and struggled to accept a god that got angry and was mean to people. Why did he hate gays and women? If I asked any questions, because I didn't understand, I got a clip round the ear. Ask again and it was a very stern response, "How dare you question the word of God?", and then a trip straight down to the headmaster's office. What a great idea! Using violence, punishment and discipline to silence the lips of the young inquisitive minds of children. That will work! That will help them learn!

Teacher: "That's how we've always done it!"
Teacher: "Well, it never did me any harm!"
Me: "Oh yes it did, sir!"

You're just repeating the bad programming you were given as a child, and you're not intelligent enough to question it. Using your train of thought, nothing would ever change. We would still have apartheid, slavery and go around burning witches!

The fact was, the priest didn't like it, because he simply couldn't answer my questions. You definitely needed to have blind faith to do well at my school, or should I say schools? I went to seven of them, eight if you include college. I spent some of my early childhood living in Africa and then once we returned to the UK, we just kept moving around a lot, but that is another story.
So I'm not saying that one thing is right and another wrong here. Some people feel they get great benefit from Catholicism. It's just that this wasn't for me. I respect all religions and everyone's right to do and believe whatever they want as long as they don't harm others.

WHAT ARE SOME OF THE DIFFERENT TECHNIQUES OF BUDDHIST MEDITATION AND HOW DOES IT WORK?

Well, there are literally hundreds!
In my Workshop 001 "An Introduction to Meditation", I go through what are called the "preliminary meditations". These are very simple to learn and a great starting point. They are like warm-up stretches for the mind. However, do not underestimate them. They are the basis for all further meditations and can be very powerful. I still use them every single day. Remember, a daily practice is essential. In the New Kadampa Tradition, you are ideally aiming for approximately fifteen minutes in the morning and then, if possible, another fifteen-minute session at night, but you can build up to this. On most retreats, however, you will meditate for much longer periods than this. It is far better than just doing reactionary meditation. A short meditation session at any given moment may help to reduce the stress at that time, but it will not develop long-lasting inner peace. With transcendental meditation, it's not optional. You must meditate for twenty minutes every morning and again for twenty minutes in the evening, no exception. This is to gain momentum and hence the full benefits of this technique. Would you take exception to breathing? TM is a very different technique to Buddhist meditation, but is also very effective. I wanted to learn this method as I felt my meditation practice had become less effective than usual and I had hit a sort of mental block, a metaphorical plateau. I was also very keen to explore new things and wanted to try this new technique as well. I had been reading about it for years. Even with meditation there will be ups and downs. The trick is to keep moving forward.

There will always be blockages and obstacles, but if you just learn to accept this as part of the process and do not resist them, they will soon dissolve. I can't go into too much detail about the TM techniques. When you go for your initial instruction, it is explained that parts of this ancient system are sacred and that you must take a vow, agreeing to keep them secret. You then sign a document to confirm you want to proceed. All of this happens prior to you engaging in your mantra ceremony. Final note on TM: it is expensive, so it's not for everyone, but if you can afford it, I would highly recommend that you give it a go! It was of great help to me and it got my meditation practice back on track. I now practice Buddhist meditation and TM every day, in the morning and then again at night. I keep both practices completely separate though. I also meditate all day, because I'm either giving workshops, doing drop-in sessions, or giving personal instruction on a one-to-one basis.

Imagine! Am I the luckiest guy in the world or what? Ommmmmmm!

If your schedule doesn't permit you to meditate in the morning and in the evening, and you have to choose between the two, then this may help you decide which will work best for you:

Morning. This is my favourite time to meditate. I like clearing my mind first and then starting the day off in the right way, with inner peace.

Evening. This is very good for emptying your head of all the day's events and activities, quieting the mind before you go to bed, and hence this improves the quality of your sleep. Letting go of your thoughts! Meditating at night really helped with my irregular sleep patterns. It enabled me to find rhythm.

> Before I started meditating, it was a very different story. Sometimes, upon awakening after a rough nights sleep, I would feel like I'd been dragged behind a car all night. Even the little amount of rest I was getting, was terrible. It's all about quality, not quantity, you see. I had neither. My mind was so busy, I felt worse after I had been to bed than when I'd had no sleep at all. This was compounded by the fact that I suffered from terrible nightmares. I think subconsciously I didn't even want to go to sleep and that was the problem. It's not a good place to be. I was living in fear and a sense of impending doom, in constant terror of the trauma that awaited me in my sleep. I knew that lurking in my mind there was always a new and even more horrific tale waiting, ready for the opportunity to come out when I closed my eyes, usually in the middle of the night ahead. Some of my nightmares were recurring, but others took me to new places, into the depths of hell. You could see why I had insomnia. Good times! I digress.

I will now talk you through four examples of preliminary meditations that I do in my Workshop 001, although I urge you to try and get down to one of the actual sessions if possible. It's so much easier to show you in person and then you are also able to ask questions as we go along.

1. **_CONCENTRATION_**

This is focusing on the breath to the exclusion of everything else.

I will use this example to explain how meditation works.
This is the most common form of meditation across the world and is used in lots of different disciplines, including yoga and various martial arts. As always, the instructions I give you here are just guidelines. Don't worry if these aren't exactly right for your practice, you can tweak them, just do whatever's comfortable. Also, that quite often, when you first start to meditate, you will feel like it's not helping at all and that it's actually making things a whole lot worse. This is not the case. It's just that you have become quiet and still. You start to look inwards and go inside. So for the first time in a very long while, perhaps ever, you will have contrast and perspective. You now become aware of how busy your mind really is, and how hectic and chaotic your thoughts are. Like a little Tasmanian devil from the cartoon _Road Runner_, your thoughts are spinning round and round, but that's the whole point. You might remember from earlier on in the book that you have to look at the problem first and become aware, in order to resolve it, even if you don't want to.

"In order to appreciate the light, you must first know the dark."—MM

A quick tangent here. "Spinning". This is the term I use to describe when you get certain persistent thoughts, going around and around, stuck in your head. It's when your mind goes into overdrive and it's exhausting. This usually happens to me after I've had a full-fat coffee. I go nuclear! I am caffeine sensitive you see. I am completely caffeine-free now.

I call decaffeinated coffee "diet coffee".
I call normal coffee "full-fat coffee".

These terms drive my mum bonkers. It's so funny. Sorry Mum. If I am in a good place inside, in bliss and fully present, I have got away with it in the past. That is, having a very small amount of caffeine. This usually only occurred when I was on holiday. If, however, I am agitated or have a very busy mind and I have a strong cup of filter coffee, RUN! Seriously, RUN! I will go berserk. One time, I was in a restaurant with two other people. I ordered and was given a diet coffee. No problem here, you say. It was delicious. You see, I do like the taste of coffee. So, as happy as a pig in poo, I then proceeded to drink large quantities of it. It then transpired that it wasn't diet coffee at all; it was in fact, a pot of very strong full-fat filter coffee. One of the waiters had given me this by mistake. I thought I was losing my mind. I felt it kick in like an atomic bomb. I was totally wired, spinning and spinning, going crazy. I was up for two days straight before I had figured out what happened. The frightening thing is when you think it's real. At least if you know you've had filter coffee and you're going mental, you know it's the coffee really. You can sort of cope mentally by just keep reminding yourself that it's the coffee and that you also know it will end. If, however, you are unaware of this detail and you have no idea what's going on, everything is real! You have crossed the road into the funny farm. You're going crazy! I felt like suing the restaurant, but it was in Rochdale and that's a long drive, so I chose the path of least resistance and managed to let it go. In my youth, I felt bulletproof and fearless, but unfortunately, I was also very angry to boot. I wouldn't have hesitated back then. I would have just gone straight back to the venue, found the waiter responsible, and committed a violent act. I would probably have given him stitches, at the very least, if not hospitalised him. Thankfully, the person I used to be no longer exists. I am very glad about this fact. He is gone for good.

Anyhow!

Start by sitting comfortably with your feet flat on the floor. Ideally, in a chair in silence. Sit with your back straight. Not straining it or sitting uncomfortably, but just upright and relaxed, keeping your spine erect. This helps you to stay focused and alert, but it also helps you to breathe properly, allowing oxygen, blood, and subtle energies to move freely and circulate around your body. Place your right hand in your left hand, touching your thumbs and then resting them in your lap. When you're ready, gently close your eyes and start to breathe in and out through your nose. When you first start to meditate, you will become aware of all the subtle sensations of your body. You will find that your ego or false self will put up a bit of a fight. Like a final struggle. It will try every trick in the book to stay in the game. It doesn't want you to take your attention inwards, to go quiet, or to become still and reconnect with your true self. Your ego wants to stay in control, and in order to do this, it will try to keep you focused outwardly, in the realm of the five senses. It will use your body to do this. This is just an initial phase of meditation and is part of the process. Imagine someone hanging on the edge of a cliff, desperately grabbing on to anything they can to stop them from falling. This is your ego. Your body is a great tool for anchoring you into this realm and for becoming fully present, for example by doing a full body scan with your mind, but this is not what we are doing in this instance. Your pants will feel too tight, your jumper will seem itchy, and you will need a wee. "But my pants weren't tight before?" In the early stages of your practice, you start to become familiar with the subtle sensations of the body. Nothing has changed except your perception and awareness. This is completely normal.

"This too shall pass!"—Ancient proverb

You see, you are about to go inside and pay a visit to a very special place indeed, to reconnect with your true self. You're going to start taking back control of your thoughts from your ego, the false self. You are going to feel empowered and then, rather than being a victim and your emotional state being controlled by external events, you will become captain of your ship, master of your destiny, and creator of your universe. Focusing on the subtle sensation of your breath, breathing in through your nose and out through your nose. At no point try to control the breath, just observe it! Fast or slow, deep or shallow, this doesn't matter; just let it be and breathe naturally. After a while, you should feel the sensation becoming stronger and your thoughts starting to reduce and subside. Your mind will then start to wander off again, with other new distracting thoughts. This is part of the meditation process. This is completely normal. Don't get frustrated. Once you realise this, just accept it and remember, you have just taken another step down the road of meditation. Every time this happens, you have moved closer to your goal. Once you become aware that your mind has moved off point, gradually bring your attention back inwards. Focus on the sensation of the breath again to the exclusion of everything else. Imagine your breath as a beautiful melody. Each time you drift away, just slowly returning to the rhythm, guiding yourself back to this heavenly harmony. No resistance, no frustration, just soft movements, back and forth. Like the ebb and flow of a gentle tide. Repeat this process again and again. After a while, you should start to feel a sense of calm, peace, and more relaxed. You are now gaining deep rest. You are learning how to go into the gap between your thoughts. This is achieved by going into the silence and becoming still.

There are two very important points to make here, crucial even.

- **There are no bad meditations.** They are all beneficial and relevant. All recognised phases and part of the process. Don't think that because you struggled and your mind was very busy, that you failed on this occasion or that it wasn't a "good one" today. All meditation is good for you and in fact, sometimes the "busy" meditations, the ones with the most distracting thoughts, can be the most beneficial of all. When you are ready, just keep returning back to the breath. This is not supposed to be a struggle or a mental wrestling match. Relax. When you have a "busy" meditation, you are releasing tension out of the body, as well as lots of stressful thoughts. This is a good thing. Don't fight it. Let it happen naturally, then gradually and gently bring your attention back to the breath once again. All sorts of random unexpected thoughts and visual special effects will probably occur during your meditation. Just observe them, but pay them no heed. Don't resist them. Just watch and then let them go!

- **Don't get frustrated!** In doing so, you can create a whole new problem, a secondary set of issues and more stressful thoughts. Don't get stressed about meditating. That would be defeating the object. Each time your mind wanders and you become aware of this, recognise it and then return your attention back to the breath, over and over. You are starting to develop a deep inner rhythm. You are starting to develop inner peace and moving towards enlightenment. You are learning how to meditate. Well done!

Remember, "Frustration is like shouting "Fire!" when you light a match; it makes a problem far bigger than it needs to be."— MM

With regular practice, this period of time, what I like to call "the wander", will start to reduce. Eventually, you will be able to concentrate exclusively on the sensation of your breath for several minutes at a time, effortlessly. You will start to develop inner peace or pure consciousness, and then learn how to take this out of the meditation and into your day. Shining your inner light, giving peace, love, and the positive energy that you are now emitting, to everyone you meet.

Later comes what they call "cosmic consciousness" in TM. This is the fifth state of consciousness. There are seven in total. Cosmic consciousness is where you stay permanently connected to pure consciousness. Simply put, pure consciousness is the place you visit in your meditation, where you feel most at peace and relaxed in the stillness. You become permanently connected to this at all times. It is with you always. You become tethered to the inner light. I will cover this in more detail later.

2. VISUALISATION

This involves using your imagination to manifest. It is having a thought about something and then holding that thought in your mind. Actually experiencing all the feelings and sensations that are associated with it in the realm of the five senses, but by going there in the mind, in the non-physical.

"The ancestor to every action is a thought!"—Ralph Waldo Emerson

"Imagination is everything. It is the preview of life's coming attractions!"—Albert Einstein

Again, focus on the breath initially, breathing in and out through the nose if comfortable to do so. Start to imagine that the outward breath is in the form of thick black smoke. Imagine this smoke being all your negative thoughts and negative energy leaving the body. Then, at the same time, imagine the inward breath in the form of a pure brilliant white light, entering and then filling up the entire body. Imagining this light being positive energy and inspiration. Repeat this pattern, with the black smoke gradually decreasing and becoming fainter and fainter, and with the white light increasing and then filling up the entire body. At the end of this meditation, all the thick black smoke has gone and the body is then completely full of pure, brilliant white light, emitting and radiating it. This is a very powerful meditation. The clever thing about this technique is that it can remove your stress and anxiety, without you even knowing exactly what is wrong in the first place. If you were agitated and feeling discomfort, this will start to dissolve. Even if you don't know what the problem is or what is bothering you, but you just feel out of sorts, this bad boy will fix it, most of the time anyway. It works wonders for me.

These first two techniques we have looked at so far are based on Buddhist meditations. They are used to clear the mind, become still and go into the silence, before advancing on to other types of meditation. With instruction you can then go on to learn such techniques as placement meditation, for example. These are much harder though and take lots of practice. Once in a relaxed state and with a clear mind, the Buddhist teacher will recite a profound text to the pupils or use one of the twenty-one Lamrim. These are the twenty-one fixed meditations, or the "quick path" from traditional Buddhist texts, to guide us to enlightenment. Once the teaching is given, or you have just read it to yourself if you're alone, we then contemplate the wisdom learned from it and a feeling is generated. This feeling is like a moment of clarity that follows, an understanding or a brief epiphany, if you will. We use this to meditate on. Focusing on the feeling generated, single-pointedly. This is called placement meditation. Each time you lose focus you have to return to the beginning. Focus on your breathing first and then, when you're ready, recite or read the teaching again. Through doing this, we regenerate the feeling, which is the focal point of the meditation. We then start the placement process once more. The preliminaries are like warm-ups, preparing the mind before the teacher gets down to serious business with the placement meditations. For most people, the preliminaries can be very powerful and are more than adequate for your daily practice. They will get you started on your meditation journey, going inside to find bliss, joy, and peace. Trust me, if you can quiet your mind and focus on your breath for even a few minutes on a regular basis, you are doing very well indeed, and you will feel huge benefits in every aspect of your life.

To learn to do the placement meditations as I did, you do need to study Buddhism really. These teachings are fixed meditations and are part of the set text. Placements are very difficult for me, and are fairly advanced stuff, so please just put them to one side for now. I can only really achieve the correct practice whilst on a retreat. When doing these, you also need to meditate for about an hour at a time, and if on retreat that is usually for five or six times a day. That's right folks, five to six hours of meditation every day.

Visualisation techniques, not just within a meditation, have been proven to work scientifically. They are so powerful that they are used by astronauts at NASA and by the US Olympic team. They use visualisation to train for their missions and events respectively. See, whether you actually do an event or you imagine going through it, you will experience it. The same electrical signals are sent, and then the same series of synapses are fired in the brain. The same thoughts are generated and the same muscles are triggered. You basically go through all of the feelings and emotions of an event, mentally and physically, as if you have actually just completed that task. The brain doesn't know the difference in that moment. They say that if you go there in the mind, you will go there in the body. I have also advised a few people who have difficulty sleeping to meditate first, of course, and then, once they get into bed, to visualise visiting their favourite holiday destination, for example. This is initially somewhere they are familiar with, somewhere they have actually been to. I tell them to try and go there in the mind, to experience the sounds, smells, colours, textures, and tastes. Not like watching this scene in a movie, but experiencing it as if they were actually there. Immerse yourself in the realm of the five senses as if you were in this place. When you are doing this, you are not thinking about work or your other problems. It is usually a very pleasant experience and you feel good. You sleep like a baby. This is also great practice; starting with the known, a place you have actually experienced and been to, and then advancing on to the unknown. This can be a place you want to go to but haven't been yet! Remember—if you go there in the mind, you will go there in the body. I could now talk about remote viewing, but I don't want your heads to fall off just yet!

3. **OBSERVATION AND AWARENESS (MINDFULNESS)**
So, what is mindfulness? It is to become aware of something. To focus your mind on one thing. To fill your mind with it. To become mind-full.

"Be mindful of your thoughts, young Padawan!"—*Star Wars: Episode 1 – The Phantom Menace*

There are two main types of mindfulness, two ways to become fully aware, and they are very different. To become mindful of action or to become mindful of thought. Essentially to become fully aware of your actions, by moving into them and immersing yourself in the realm of the five senses, or to become fully aware of your thoughts, by stepping back, moving away from them, and observing them in your mind.

- **Mindfulness of action**—this is what Zen Buddhists do, as I mentioned earlier. They immerse themselves fully in any action they are doing, experiencing every feeling, sound, touch, smell, and taste. They do this in lots of ways, but also in their Japanese tea ceremony. By doing this, they become fully present and are completely in the moment. Their thoughts are aligned with the now.

I recently took part in a mindfulness class in Touchstones Art Gallery in Rochdale.

I also teach there. This class was led by my friend Lisa, who works there. I call her the boss but she says she's not. I did this class just to try it out and see what it was like. You see, I normally teach and practice the latter of the two, mindfulness of thought—moving away from thought by using mental observation techniques. The class was wonderful. We would choose a piece of art to focus on and then each try to experience every detail of that artwork fully, as a group, in silence. It was fascinating, because when we discussed it afterwards, we had all picked up different details from it, some that I had missed. Even though we were doing the same thing, in the same place, we all relayed a completely different evaluation. It's all down to interpretation. I thoroughly enjoyed the class and would recommend that everyone gives it a whirl. As with all meditation, even guided in a group setting and all doing the same technique, as this class illustrates, it is a very personal journey. After all, we are going inwards, and even though we are all connected, we are all individuals and completely unique. All meditations start with instruction and are guided initially. Just like driving lessons, we need these to get going, but then we are off, exploring on our own. Ideally, we need someone to discuss the experiences with and answer questions as we go along. This would be what they call "sangha" in Buddhism, one of the three jewels. This means community or assembly and refers to the nuns and monks that help us. Basically, from here on in, you are pioneers, exploring your own minds. It is a place that is only accessible by the self and so is just for you. The final frontier, if you will. It is a very exciting and beautiful experience to undertake. Look inside, for all the answers lie within. Go there and see!

- **Mindfulness of thought**—so this is the one I teach in my workshops. This is the third meditation. We will meditate as usual by initially focusing on the breath to the exclusion of everything else, except this time, we actually observe our thoughts. Without engaging them, we just let them be, occurring naturally, and then watch them pass by. With this method, each time a thought should appear, we imagine it in the form of a little white cloud, gradually floating by and then disappearing into the distance. We don't engage the thought and we don't react to the thought, we just leave it alone and watch it drift past. When we observe our thoughts, just by this act, we create separation. If I see you over there and I am over here, then logically you are not me. So by observing a thought, we create space between us and it. We recognise it as a thought and therefore as a separate entity, and then, in most cases, we are able to let it go by using this visualisation technique.

For example, anger!
All feelings such as anger are generated by our thoughts. So instead of "being" angry and immersed in an angry feeling, we learn to pause. With inner peace, we develop the skills and calmness required to dissect this process. Recognising an angry thought before it has lit the fire. In this simple step, we realise that we are not angry. It is just an angry thought.
We learn to observe it and remember we all have these, so there's no shame or frustration here.
Within just a brief moment, we can identify it as unwanted and stop the usual process in its tracks. We start to change the pattern. We start to re-programme. We let it pass and choose not to pick it up. We decide that it is simply a negative thought and a separate entity. It is not required, it does not serve us, and we don't need it. It is not our true self or our true nature. It is born from an uncontrolled mind and incorrect thought. We then just relax, observe it with no resistance, and let it float past. It gradually dissolves and then disappears off into the distance. Simples!

I am not angry! I just had an angry thought and I chose to let it go. That's all!

4. **VOCALISATION (USING MANTRA)**

Now, mantra can be used both internally, recited repeatedly over and over again in the mind, and externally. In this section I am going to talk specifically about the external use of mantra that we usually do in my introduction workshops. If we have time at the end of the session, I like to cover this fourth meditation. So far, all the meditations have been quiet, internalised with no sound. I like to finish a class with chanting, using a chosen mantra. Done as a group, this is amazing and a very powerful experience. I love doing this! It generates a lot of joy. That's right folks, vocalising a sound externally. I tell everyone that it doesn't matter what they sound like. It doesn't matter about their breathing and it doesn't matter if they want to laugh. Just relax, do it, and enjoy it.

> I have one particular man that comes to my house for regular private lessons (I do a few of these in special cases) and he just can't stop laughing. This in turn makes me laugh. He brings me more pleasure than he could possibly realise. After all, his natural state is joy.
>
> I remember being in church as a child and if you started laughing (I did this regularly) you got in a lot of trouble and thrown out! I would then be in a state of dread and terror on the car journey home, because I knew what was coming! Imagine a child getting into trouble for experiencing joy. I'm just talking about laughing for "God's" sake. Maybe even take me outside to laugh my head off and let me get it out of

my system, but not to be punished. There was something about not being able to laugh in certain environments, mass in this instance, which made it so much funnier and made me want to do it even more. Although I did think that going to church was very funny anyway! Suppressing joy is bad programming. I think we all take life way too seriously. We need to be able to find, and then see the humour in every situation. It's especially important to learn to laugh at ourselves.

Did you know that the average child laughs more than three hundred times a day? And, wait for it, the average adult just fifteen. Yes, you heard me correctly. Fifteen! Again, this is down to bad programming. The system squeezes the life out of kids as they are growing up. By the time we reach puberty, we are usually highly stressed, confused, and things just aren't quite as funny anymore. Life, and the programming we are given, gets dead serious.

Anyway, we were chanting. I tell everyone to make sure that they close their eyes and then just to follow my lead. Then panic sets in. I can see it in everyone's eyes. They are getting a little bit outside their comfort zone. I can't sing? What if I sound terrible? What if I get it wrong? What if I'm out of time? I explain to everyone that we will use the mantra "Om" in this session, as it is a very simple mantra to begin with, but yet also very powerful. Om is the mantra of everything. This vibrational frequency is found throughout nature. It is the sound of the universe and in all things. In Buddhism we use "Om Mani Padme Hum" a lot, but this is much harder to get comfortable with on your first go at chanting. The translation is roughly "jewel in the lotus" but the simple meaning of this mantra is "a wish to end all suffering". This word is Sanskrit, one of the oldest languages known to man from Medieval India; it is still used in both Buddhism and Hinduism today. I also use mala beads to count the repetitions of the mantra. In Buddhism, we have 108 beads on a string of mala beads. You will see these worn around the necks of many practising Buddhists. They are very similar to Catholic rosary beads or Islamic prayer beads. In Buddhism, we also do everything in multiples of three. I think this is mainly because of the three jewels, but there are many other reasons for this. These three jewels are:

1. Buddha—the awakened one.
2. Dharma—the teachings of Buddha in this case.
3. Sangha—the Buddhist communities. These are made up of the nuns and monks in centres up and down the country who practice the teachings of Buddha.

So off I go, chanting away. I start and then most people, after a minute or so, join in and start to chant too. After all, what have you got to lose? It's all in divine order, and besides, everything is just a dream anyway! After a short period of time, everyone has settled in and you would be surprised, we usually harmonise without any planning or discussion. The sound is beautiful. We also naturally start to synchronise, so all our breathing is in time.

We are now as a group, matching the frequency of the universe, resonating with it and sending out peace and love. Perfect! Then comes the fun part: I deliberately throw in a "long Om". I told you, this is great! I can hold an Om for a minute or so, because I have practiced it many times. This causes chaos. Everyone is now out of sync, the breathing doesn't match anymore, and the Oms are all over the place. It's heavenly carnage, but still very beautiful. There are quite often fits of giggles at this point. Some people try to match my long Om and then get short of breath. I did tell them not to. Others start Oming really fast. You see, although pleasant to harmonise and synchronise, the frequency of your Oms are yours alone. I did tell everyone that the sound they made and the rhythm of their breathing didn't matter before we started. After the long Om, I then return to shorter, medium-length Oms, and as if by magic, everything falls back into place. We all begin to synchronise again and then harmonise once more. Now, just to be clear, I don't want you to think that I am being cruel or teasing anyone. This variation is done intentionally and for good reason. There is a very important lesson to be learnt in this simple exercise. You need to be able to sing your own song regardless of the external circumstances. It's your journey, your life to live, and your dharma to follow. You have to be yourself, following your own path and singing your song. Don't blindly follow the crowd. You don't have to fit in, and it doesn't matter what other people say or do. You are perfect exactly as you are. You have divinity within you!

Remember, "If you follow your own path, you can't get lost! When you're a pioneer, there is no map."—MM

There is nothing wrong with enjoying what you do, especially if it has a valuable message within. I have a lot of fun with this and by all accounts, everyone else does too. It's amazing how my life has changed. I am getting my kicks from long Oms now instead of chemicals. I also like to "linger longer" and "Sharm Hurghada", but that's another story. Everyone has a great big smile on their face at the end of this meditation; it's beautiful and fun. A room full of smiles—I must be doing something right. I've had a couple of ladies crying at the end of this kind of meditation too, but they weren't tears expressing sadness, they were tears of relief. Something significant had happened. Some long-held suppressed emotions had come to the surface and these feelings were released. Their energy had shifted and they were experiencing joy.

OM MANI PADME HUM

Unwinding moments in silence,

Unlocking thoughts that you find.

Beyond the invisible feelings,

and the freedom within your mind.

To feel each thought you're thinking,

to let your journey begin.

To travel beyond inner-vision,

On your spiritual pathways within.

Our circle of life goes on turning,

Healing the pain that we find.

Shedding light on invisible journeys,

As the pathways of life unwind.

Each heart beat measured moment,

Each journey you begin.

Each faded breath you're breathing out,

Each breath you're breathing in.

As silence fills the empty void,

We feel the dawning sun.

And peaceful rhythms serenade,

Om Mani Padme Hum.

A poem by my friend, D.W. Parry.

This piece was actually written during one of my meditation sessions. Don regularly appears at my classes, reading poetry and singing for us. Thank you, Don.

"If we all Om together, we will have peace forever." —MM

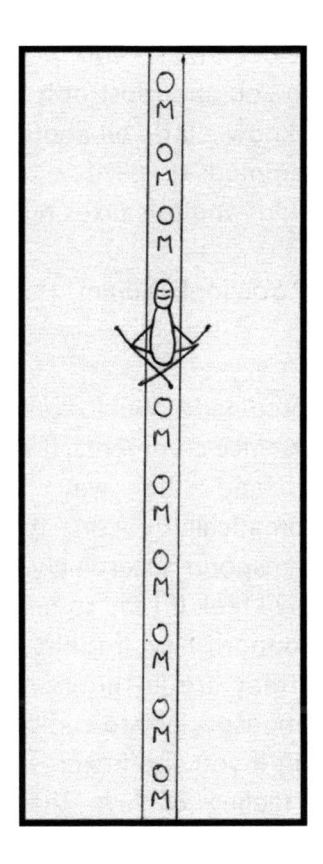

"OM...OM...OM...OM...OM..."

SOUND

This is a wonderful medium and a valuable tool that can be used in meditation, but also in many other ways too. Sound can be used to heal. I can make you feel good with sound. I can say something to you and most of it is probably true, but this is also because I know a little bit about your programming. See, we are programmed to elicit a specific response to certain external stimulus and this takes our power away.

"How are you today? You look radiant! Have you lost weight? I love your dress!"

Boom! I'm getting homemade chilli for tea tonight!
See, although they are nice comments, it is actually because of your programming and the way your mind works subconsciously. Automatically reacting to a compliment, you then think, feel and respond accordingly. By the way, I don't do this; I only say how I feel. If I say something nice, I mean it! Whenever I get the opportunity, if I think something pleasant about a person and they are in the vicinity, I say something and relay this to them, especially to complete strangers. What a waste of a lovely gift if you don't express it. A little pocket of positive energy, a feeling of love that you've generated internally through thought and then you share it with someone. How simple and yet amazing is that? It is the kind of thinking that, with the corresponding action, can light up the world. Get out of your comfort zone and grow a pair. If you see that someone is "shining" when you walk past, tell them. You might never see them again, but you may have just changed their life. For in that moment, you have lifted their

spirit and given them bliss, for free. You just made their day. Maybe they were on their way to an interview and ended up getting the job they applied for, just because they were so happy and pleasant, emitting a beautiful energy to everyone around them. Maybe they meet a fellow commuter that day, who said hello for the first time because they were so radiant and joyful, and that person turned out to be the love of their life. All this could happen as a direct result of what you say to someone. Or maybe they just go and share that bliss with everyone they meet in their day. Can you see? You are changing the world, lifting the energy and raising the consciousness of the planet, one person at a time. You have made it a better place to be! Go on, do it!

Just by using sound, my words for instance, in most cases I can instigate a chosen emotional reaction inside your mind and hence your body also. So I can make you feel good, but I can also make you feel bad. People can use this power to hurt someone or try to instigate a negative response and control you. This is where inner peace, the deep lake, comes into play. Your inner peace is your force field against other people's negative energies; it is your protective layer that dissolves lower frequencies emitted towards you. This is why the state of mind of an athlete before and during an event is crucial.

For example:

There is a notorious battle that goes on between boxers before a fight, called a "grudge match". By instigating an emotional response from your opponent prior to an event, you can disturb their rhythm. You can affect their inner peace and cause them to experience anger or anxiety, which distracts them from their goal and also wastes lots of energy and adrenaline. It takes their focus off the job in hand. This is commonly referred to as "psyching someone out".

"Keep your eyes on the prize."
"Don't let him get inside your head."
"His head's not in the game."
"His head's gone."

Also, for example, in golf, the whole game is reliant on a player being focused, calm, and relaxed. This means that as a player, all your muscles need to be relaxed to swing the club. You can't even hit the ball properly if you are tense. It is impossible to "swing" the club correctly. If you have stressful thoughts in your mind, then you have the corresponding tension in your body. It completely ruins your performance for a while, and unless you can clear your mind and regain your composure, your round goes down the pan.

You need to be aware of, but not controlled by, external events. You, and you alone, are in charge of your thoughts, feelings, and inner emotional state. Remember to stop for a moment and be independent of the good opinion of others. Act, don't react. This involves a brief pause before you choose what to do and how to respond, if at all. This way, you are not just automatically matching the low frequency and negative energy that is given to you. You will then feel empowered. You can choose not to respond at all, or to do so with a much higher frequency, love. No confrontation and no resistance.

You can dissolve most negative energies and situations by simply not resisting them. In doing so, they become irrelevant, and without opposition they just disappear. You don't feed them. What you focus on, you give your energy to. For conflict to exist there has to be opposition. There has to be two sides. Just refuse to be one of them.

Remember, "Whatever you focus on, you feed and move towards it."—MM

So you don't have to feel bad if someone says something unpleasant towards you and you don't have to get angry when someone is rude or pushes in. Yes, that's right, folks, you heard me correctly. You heard it here: being offended is a choice and therefore optional. This may seem strange or even impossible at first, but once you have developed inner peace through meditation, this gets a whole lot easier. You start to recognise people that don't match your frequency; you become very aware of them because you have contrast. You will then find that you encounter these people far less often, and when you do, they are much easier to manage. Imagine being able to take away the power from others to control you, deciding instead to take charge of your thoughts and hence how you are going to feel. Well, if you didn't realise it already, it's right there waiting for you. The controls are in your hands and you are driving. If you develop inner peace and correct thought, through a regular meditation practice, you can take charge of how you feel.

"You're the MD of your thoughts and the CEO of your inner peace. It's your business!"—MM

You have been in charge all along, always in the driving seat, but you just didn't know how to operate the controls properly. Imagine pushing a car down a hill and then jumping in with no idea how to use it. You would be at the mercy of the ground ahead, boulders, craters, and maybe even a cliff edge. You are probably going to crash, even if you can see things coming beforehand; you are helpless and unable to change course. Once you learn how to think correctly and stay peaceful, you can avoid most of life's obstacles.

By the way, if you want to help someone, never lower your frequency to match theirs, always try and lift them up to match yours. You don't want to resonate with their lower frequency, rather give them the option to raise theirs to a higher level, to resonate with you. You don't want to feel suffering as they do. More sadness never resolves it. Instead, you want them to feel joy like you do. Invite them up to see the view. Some people aren't ready to rise yet, but that is their choice. All you can do is show them the path, even offer to hold their hand along the way if you like, but only they can walk it.

Sound is a very powerful medium. It can harm someone if used incorrectly, but it can also heal if used in the right way. Just think how certain pieces of music make you feel and how they can lift your mood. I have recently started going to gong baths. I have been to seven now. Wow. They are amazing. I have been attending the Harmony Hub in Chorley, a wonderful spiritual community. At this venue, each individual gong has a name. They are all named after the planets, Earth, Jupiter, Saturn, etc. You can also attend a sound bath which is similar to a gong bath, but instead they use a whole host of other instruments as well, such as Tibetan singing bowls and bells. We will just stick to the gong bath for my purposes here though. All the gongs make a different sound and hence emit a different frequency. You can sit or, as I prefer to, lie down on a mat, in a room full of people. Then you close your eyes and off you go. You are taken on a journey into sound, immersing yourself in the magical waves and rhythms, but you don't just hear the gongs, you feel them! They are a very powerful instrument and you can literally feel the sound waves vibrating your body. Each gong has a different sound and hence a different frequency. The various gongs can match the frequencies of different parts of your body and resonate with them. Now, whether it's realigning your chakras, releasing trapped energies, or purging old emotions, you can call it what you want, but great healing can occur. For most people, their first gong bath is emotional, clearing blockages and releasing trapped energies. These could be from their past, the consequences of negative life experiences that they may have been carrying around with them for years. Just imagine vibrating something under water and then watching all the trapped air bubbles being released and rising to the surface. This is sort of what happens to your body. It's a must. Stick it on your bucket list.

WHAT ARE THE PHYSICAL BENEFITS OF MEDITATION?

Well, this is a seriously big list. Once you develop inner peace and then start to take this out of your meditation and into your daily routine, the benefits start to unfold in every direction. They pervade into every aspect of your life. I generally use the term "inner peace", but I will just flip to the TM terms here for a minute, as they are easier to explain and understand. A practitioner of TM would say that you visit pure consciousness every time you meditate.

Remember, "Ten minutes in the bank, all day at the market."—Maharishi Mahesh Yogi, when referring to the benefits of regular transcendental meditation.

You then take this peaceful state, this pure consciousness, out of your meditation (the bank), and use it during the course of your day (the market).

The fifth level of consciousnesses is called "cosmic consciousness".

Awake, asleep, deep sleep, pure consciousness, and then cosmic consciousness. There are seven levels of consciousness in total. With cosmic consciousness, however, there is a subtle difference. Rather than just taking the benefits of pure consciousness from your meditation out into your day, the door stays open and you stay connected to the source the whole time. Imagine that you have your big toe permanently dipped into pure consciousness. It has a huge effect on your life. Like an ocean, if a drop of water is disconnected, it is isolated, alone, and has no power. However, put that drop of water back into the sea and keep it permanently connected to that system, immersed in and flowing with the nature of that ocean, then it has immense power. It has the power to move mountains. It is being reconnected to the unified field and hence everything in the universe. If that drop of water is riding on the crest of a wave, fully present and in the now if you will, it will experience life to its fullest potential, in bliss and joy, because it is following its dharma. Surfing through life, in harmony with natural law. Epic! What a ride!

So, I am going to list just a few of the benefits of meditation here, starting with the physical:

- You gain deep rest during the actual meditation. It is said that twenty minutes practicing TM can be the equivalent to having several hours of sleep.
- You sleep better and this has a positive effect on your whole body.
- You start to dream a lot. Your subconscious does some long overdue de-cluttering.
- You have much more energy and because you're not as tired, you are nicer to be around, not as irritable and snappy.

- You're nicer to be around and so consequently your relationships start to improve.
- Your body heals better, much more quickly, and your immune system improves.
- Your nervous system starts to function normally because you are not permanently stressed and anxious.
- You are more relaxed and start to become fully present more often and so you have fewer accidents.
- You have more energy so your diet improves because you don't need all that refined sugar and caffeine. You can still have these items, you just don't need them as much, because you don't get the energy spikes and slumps as you did before.
- You need less Big Pharma and drugs because you feel good. To be clear, I'm not suggesting that you stop all prescription drugs overnight! I stopped drinking regularly without even trying. I just didn't feel like it or enjoy it anymore.
- You are happy and getting healthier.

The body is a self-healing miracle machine and if nurtured properly, given the correct rest, exercise, fuel, and mental environment, it starts to heal. It has boundless energy and a sense of feeling fantastic. When you start to follow your dharma, your cells start to follow theirs. They just want to heal, grow, and regenerate. Cooperating and serving you as part of a harmonious system. Your body can heal almost anything given half a chance. Miracles happen every day.

"Your miracles are an inside job."—Dr Wayne Dyer

So we haven't covered the mental or spiritual benefits yet. This list is just a few of the benefits to the body. Some of the physical benefits appear in the list of mental benefits too, as they overlap.

WHAT ARE THE MENTAL BENEFITS OF MEDITATION?

This list contains just some of the mental benefits that you will experience.
These include:

- Improved clarity, concentration, and focus.
- Increased creativity.
- Better discipline and willpower if required. Things just get a whole lot easier.
- Better decision-making ability. You start making better choices based on factors like: Does this make me feel good? And is this good for me? Eventually asking, is this good for humanity?
- When you feel good and have lots of energy, you don't eat as much refined sugar and processed food. You don't need the chemical energy boosts as much. As a result you have less mood swings. Your diet just starts to improve naturally. You generally don't want to put a greasy burger and fries into your body when you are feeling this good.
- You develop acceptance. You decide to stop worrying about things you have no control over.
- You make decisions quickly without overthinking everything.
- You make far less decisions based on financial gain, realising that you simply don't need more useless material possessions.
- You go to bed earlier because you're excited about the next day, so you get more rest.

- You have more free time because you are so much more efficient. You actually get more done in less time because you are assertive. As such, you finish your jobs much sooner and so have more time to relax and just be. You can see that this cycle perpetuates. It increases and magnifies. The more you feel good, the more you do well, and then the more good things happen to you too. The universe is just an outward expression of your inner world. A big cosmic mirror.

"When you do good, you feel good!"—MM

- Improved memory
- Renewed access to memories long since buried or forgotten, from your childhood or many years ago.
- Obviously you are now calmer, more relaxed, peaceful, and less stressed.
- Difficult situations become easier or just dissolve altogether.
- You start to hang about with positive people and attract them into your life. Those that are on the same frequency as you.

I personally had lots of other amazing things happen to me. I became vegetarian and then vegan! I had an appointment to have a cyst surgically removed from my back, after being there for years and constantly growing, it just packed its bags and went on holiday. "Ecky-thump!"

I had both knees heal, after being told multiple surgeries were the only option. I was told that I wouldn't be able to run and that I may not even be able to go walking again. No surgery, and now completely healed. By the way, did I mention that I am an Iron Man? Haha!

I had constant issues with neck pain, which is now manageable without drugs for pain relief, and so my quality of life has improved immeasurably. I just need to look straight ahead all the time though! Maybe there is another lesson in there for me! Haha!

I could go on. I dare you to try it and see what miracles await you.

By the way, if you do eat meat, that's your choice. I might want to eat a piece too at some point. It's completely up to you. I may not choose to eat meat, but that is my choice and up to me. If you are vegan, and one time you don't feel well, you are weak and need a boost of vitamin B12, and you eat some meat, this doesn't mean you're evil. You're not going to hell. You're not going to be cast out onto the streets by the Vegan Mafia. Remember, we can't have world peace if everyone's not invited. This means the application of acceptance. We have to practice non-judgement and forgiveness, starting with ourselves.

"Not Buddha yet!"—*Chicken Soup for the Soul*

We just have guidelines to work with; ideals to move towards, and then you just do your best. That's it. I constantly make mistakes and get things wrong. I still make bad decisions, just much less than I used to.

Remember, "What you think of me is none of my business."—Dr Wayne Dyer

You see, if this were true and the Vegan Mafia were right (and I have met them, by the way) then we're all stuffed. I would not want to be a vegan by their definition.

Remember, "To err is human; to forgive, divine."—Alexander Pope

See, following this logic:

Catholics would be thrown out of the church if they missed mass or confession once, and that is basically all Catholics. The religion would be finished overnight.

Buddhists would be thrown out of the temple because they had a glass of wine, a cigarette, or a burger one time, and again, that's basically every Buddhist I have ever met. I don't mean they did all three things regularly or at once, I just mean one of them occasionally.

With this reasoning, I would have to fire myself! You're sacked, Midnight! You're not pretending to be perfect! You're disrupting the system! You are questioning the bad programming and the lie! "Meditations by Midnight" says you're fired! But my name's in the company title? Well, we will just change it then to, ermmm..., to Sunset.

Yes, "Meditations by Sunset". Who the hell is Sunset? And why haven't I met her before? Actually, that does sound a bit better, in fact...oh dear! Sod it! That's my new name now, it's Sunset McBride! I'm going to have to grow my hair long now, so I look the part! I'm on a tangent again. I love tangents!

So you see, we are not perfect, or at least not as the system and media portray us anyway, but we are all in fact perfect creations. We come from and are still connected to divine intelligence. We just need to open the door and look inwards.

Remember, "We are not human beings having a spiritual experience; we are spiritual beings having a human experience."—Dr Wayne Dyer

Forgiveness starts from within. We need to forgive ourselves first, for not being what we cannot be, false idols.

"Forgiveness is the fragrance that the violet sheds on the heel that has crushed it."—Mark Twain

This is, in my opinion, one of the most beautiful quotes ever written.

In fact, this is one of the main issues in society today: people are not willing to admit that they are flawed and make mistakes. We need to talk about everything. We need to break the cycle. We must start by sharing the lessons we have learnt with others, passing on the valuable information from our experiences and breaking the old repeating patterns. Questioning the bad programming we have been given by our system. We need to be honest with ourselves and with each other. Then we can improve our situation. It's up to us. Only then are we able to raise the level of human consciousness, all emitting and operating at a higher frequency, love! The more perfect someone pretends to be, the perfect that is portrayed in the media, the more insecure they usually are and the more issues they probably have. Masking all their problems, or better still, let's call them "challenges". They are all hiding behind a facade, burying all the things we really need to address, beneath layer upon layer of lies. Often not just convincing others of their nonsense, they start to believe it themselves. If I hadn't made loads of mistakes, and I mean loads, I wouldn't have learned a damn thing.

"Before every major success come many minor failures."— MM

"In order to be the most improved, you have to start at the bottom. To be truly remarkable, you must first be truly terrible. This is growth. This is progress. This is evolution!"— MM

"If I could go back, would I do things differently? Yes, of course. I have evolved and grown. So do you regret anything? No, of course not. That's how I have evolved and grown."—MM

We need to have contrast to know what it is to feel good. I make lots of mistakes, but this is still progress. They are not really errors, but instead lessons. We gain valuable information on our life journey, and then use this to fine tune our heading, as a guidance system to plot a new course. Our intuition is like God talking to us. Decisions made by using our feelings and intuition as a compass, with the right motivation, are nearly always good ones. Things either go well or we learn a very important lesson. Just keep moving forward. Don't stagnate from fear. Everything in a stagnant pond dies. We need energy, our life blood, flowing through us to grow. Regularly and intentionally address fear. Step outside your comfort zone. Learn to embrace change and experience new things. How can we expect to grow and see positive results if we don't step outside the old framework?

"If you don't make changes, you will never see change!"—MM

We have to let go of the old, cast it off and cut it loose. Only then can we make room for the new and start to make progress. It's exhausting being stressed all the time, feeling remorse, regret, and guilt. Throw it away! Let it go. What have you got to lose?

"Let go and let God."—Dr Wayne Dyer

I know I have said this before, but there is in fact one thing we definitely all have in common: we are all broken. These cracks, however, can be a blessing; they unlock and then open doorways into the spirit realm and the divine. I am not saying we should seek out suffering, far from it, but if we don't want the cycle to keep repeating, we must learn from it. We must evolve. Only then will we know peace.

Remember, "We are all broken. That's how the light gets in."—Ernest Hemingway

"You have to keep breaking your heart until it opens."—Rumi

"The wound is the place where the light enters you."—Rumi

"Through adversity and trauma comes peace. We can then open new doors and experience the divine."—MM

WHAT ARE THE SPIRITUAL BENEFITS?

These are infinite and I definitely don't have all the answers yet; I haven't got to the end of my journey.

"A man who thinks he knows everything knows very little. A man who realises how little he knows may know something!"—MM

Every day I learn something new. My life is full of wonder now and I see beauty where before there was none. Every day is a new adventure. I am excited to be alive again. Can you remember being a child, when everyday was like one big holiday? Waking up at 5 a.m. because you were so excited you could wee. Not wanting to go to bed because you didn't want the day to end.

My mum: "What's all the noise about? It's 5 a.m.!"

Me: "I know, Mum, but it's Wednesday!"

My mum: "What is so special about Wednesday?"

Me: "It's a brand new day, Mum! We can do anything!"

When you meditate regularly, develop inner peace, and become fully present, there are some significant spiritual benefits.

For example, life gets a whole lot easier. You start to see lots of subtle changes everywhere and some great big whoppers too! No Burger King here thanks! Where there were problems, there are less. Where there was drama, there is less. Slowly, all resistance starts to fall away and gradually disappears altogether, and then magic starts to happen. Here are two ways you will notice it:

1. **You start to see beauty all around you.**

Beauty in the people you meet, beauty in the people that you have known all along, beauty in life, and especially beauty in nature! Everything changes. You start to see the good in every situation, and if you really can't see any, then that person or situation either slowly moves away from you of their own accord or just vanishes. You see they don't match your frequency anymore. They don't resonate with you, and after all, the universe is just a mirror.

"In Lak'ech" is a Mayan greeting and means "You are another me!" We are all one. One tribe, one universe, one song.

I have this phrase tattooed on my body. I have hundreds of words in ink all over my skin and lots of artwork too. I haven't counted them for a long time, but there are many and they are still growing. They used to call me "quote man" in the local tattoo shop.

My back is completely covered in positive phrases and sayings. If I meet you one day, I will happily show you. There are many stories behind these. I see tattoos as a means of expression, like external emotional scars. Quite beautiful in some cases, but not all. For me, whenever something significant happens in my life, I get a tattoo, so they all have meaning. Sometimes it is about a shift in the way I am thinking or feeling, not always an actual external event.

2. Synchronicity (coincidences—there aren't any!)

These will start to pop up constantly, every day. Once you slow down and start to look with better eyes, you start to see "coincidences" everywhere. They are all around you. They have always been there, but you were either going too fast to notice or you just weren't looking. Carl Jung would call this "synchronicity" and Ester Hicks would call it "alignment".

This is an analogy I like to use a lot. If you're driving to Blackpool and you're on the wrong road, you won't see any signs. Similarly, if you're driving too fast on the right road or not looking where you are going, you won't see them either. However, if you're driving on the right road and you slow down a bit and look around, you will see signs for Blackpool every step of the way. If you haven't got it, the signposts are "coincidences" and the road you're on is your current life journey. The correct road is your dharma, your spiritual path. When you follow this you will see "the signs" everywhere. This especially applies to crossroads or junctions in your life, major decisions you have to make, when you need directions and signposts the most. You need to stop and take a good look around before deciding which way to go and which road to choose. Don't be confused though, this does not mean overthinking everything. It simply means having a clear mind when you need to focus and choose. So when I have a big decision to make, this is what I do. I meditate, become still, and go into the gap. I let the sediment fall to the riverbed, and my busy daily thoughts subside. This is so I have clarity and I can see clearly. I then have a moment. I become aware of my subtle energies and feelings inside. Only after this do I decide on the correct course of action. I don't do this for every decision I make or I would never be able to leave the house, although I do sometimes decide to stay at home and meditate some more! I just apply this for the big stuff though, when I'm not sure what to do. Through remaining calm and having clarity from your meditation, you are able to be assertive. You start to feel like you are actually driving the car for the first time and not just a passenger in it or worst still, being dragged behind it in a dustbin.

This analogy can also be applied to your life prior to awakening. If you want to go to Blackpool, but are on the wrong road heading to Chester, you won't see any of the signs for the "Pleasure Beach". Worse still, there are no junctions coming up ahead, so you are trapped going the wrong way and can't get off the highway. Sound familiar? You're running out of fuel and will eventually have a "breakdown". If you just stop suddenly in the middle of the motorway, there will be a pile up. Your wife, kids, and all the family that rely upon you are passengers in the car. The service station is the only brief respite you can take. It's the only place you can go for now. This is where you can refuel and rest briefly. This is like going on a holiday for two weeks of the year or doing something you enjoy as a distraction, like shopping. When you have discord and imbalance in your life, it can feel like this. You need to get off at the first junction, rather than moving further away from your destination and then ending up like me, having a real life breakdown because you ran out of fuel. Gradually start moving out of the fast lane into the slow lane and eventually getting off that road altogether. Far better to choose a spiritual awakening, starting to follow your dharma, rather than to be thrown off life's merry-go-round. Just like a hamster on a wheel, when it's running at full tilt and then suddenly stops, the momentum of the wheel sends him flying through the air. We are all like this before the shift. In some cases, literally. Just drive through Manchester town centre at teatime and look at all the people in health clubs. You can see them in the tower blocks, through the big glass windows, running on treadmills in the gyms. They could be outside running. We need help. Let's get off the wheel.

So, to experience synchronicity, a quick recap: initially, you start to become aware and then quiet your mind. You are aligned with the present moment, in the now, and you develop inner peace. You then start to notice the subtle inner sensations of your body, your feelings and intuition, and you use these tools for guidance and decision making. This is instead of the usual warped logic derived from bad programming. You then start to follow your path. You move in the direction of things that make you feel good, that are without drama, that just flow effortlessly, and the entire universe starts to cooperate with you and your purpose. You are moving in harmony and without resistance. You have arrived. You are now following your dharma.

Remember, "The universe will correspond to the nature of your song."—Reverend Dr Michael Beckwith

This is when things start to get a whole lot easier. You get exactly what you want and exactly what you need, at exactly the right moment, just in the nick of time. People start to show up just at the right time, when maybe you need a helping hand. Money appears, just when you have to pay a bill. This is because you are working in harmony with natural law. Just like all animals, plants, and other living things that occur in nature, you are following your dharma. You are now in tune with your own nature and operating naturally. You are moving in the same direction as life, with the flow of the universe and its energy, not resisting and swimming against it. You are going downstream and applying almost no effort. You are being carried by God. As long as your motivations are good and you get your negative thought patterns out of the way, everything you need will appear before you, at your feet. Your life will start to unfold in front of you effortlessly, without struggle. You will start to manifest not occasionally, but every day. It will become normal for you to experience the miraculous. You will feel inspired and empowered.

Many people that achieved something great in their lives will tell you, they didn't really do anything. They simply let God in. Human beings' thought patterns can be like a circuit breaker, stopping the flow of life. These people simply got out of the way and allowed the universe, God, or "the force", if you like, to flow through them. They were a conduit, a vessel, a channel!

This is one of the qualities of a "self-actualised person" according to Maslow.

Other significant spiritual effects, which are very profound, that you will start to notice when you meditate regularly are:

You will become very aware of the subtle sensations of the body and also your energy levels and the things that affect it, like other peoples energies, especially if they are very different from yours. Feeling the frequencies they emit, their emotional needs, wants, and even demands.

You will also start to dream a lot. I always used to dream a lot anyway, before I started to meditate, but as you now know, they were dark twisted nightmares. These post-meditation dreams though are usually incredibly vivid, beautiful and breathtaking. I have had some experiences of being surrounded by pure love, flying through the night sky with kindred spirits and multicoloured beings of light. I have been laughing all night long, having fun with transvestite clowns, on the trapeze in a circus. Dancing with people on the street in a musical, and then writing the lyrics from that song when I woke up from the dream. I have also been to Robin Hood's wedding in a forest, floating above them during the ceremony, being able to smell the wet leaves and wild flowers.

This is way better than watching television, don't you think?

You see, your mind, under the correct circumstances and conditions, is an amazing tool. It has limitless potential for you to explore, once you open the door, if you dare?

The last topic I will cover here is knowing. Imagine if you knew everything was going to be okay. That you could use your special powers to look forward in time and could see that everything works out just fine. Well, that's sort of what you get. You don't just believe you actually know that everything is going to be okay, that everything is exactly as it should be and that everything is in divine order. Well then, there is just no need to worry. You are a perfect piece of an intelligently designed system, divine in nature and operating in harmony within natural law. No mistakes. You are perfect. There are no mistakes in nature. God doesn't make mistakes. If you are following your true nature, thinking correctly and following your dharma, you are operating as part of this system. All the fear and doubt will gradually dissolve from your mind and all that's left is peace, love, and light. That's what I know! Oh, and if it's not alright, then that's alright too; don't forget, it's all just a dream anyway!

"Everything's going to be alright!" —*No Woman No Cry* by Bob Marley

I call this F.A.I.T.H.

(This is my alter ego. I am "Faith Harmony". This is my pseudonym, which I use when I'm performing as drag queen at the weekends. Just teasing. Although I do like to put a dress on every now and again, it's so liberating though, not having to wear a bra all the time.)

Freedom And Inspiration Through Harmony.

This is you, positive energy moving forward, with your mind thinking correctly, following your inspired thoughts and intuition. You then start experiencing freedom by transcending fear, following your dharma and operating within natural law. Thus, having no resistance and working in harmony. If you apply everything I have talked about, you will become F.A.I.T.H.

Note that you don't have F.A.I.T.H., you become it!

If you think correctly, self-generating positive energy, and then start listening to your feelings using them as your compass, you are motoring. Then, doing what makes you feel good, you will start moving along the right tracks. You will start to follow your dharma and move forward with no resistance, experiencing the miraculous and the divine.

Once you become F.A.I.T.H, you will become streamlined, like an arrow flying through the air. Nothing will be impossible. You will have unlimited potential and know God. You will then also know that everything is going to work out just fine. God is divine intelligence and he is in you.

"If you knew who walks beside you on this path that you have chosen, fear would be impossible." —*A Course in Miracles*

I still have ups and downs. I have good days and occasionally not-so-good days, but very rarely bad days. I still have fluctuations, but they are at a higher level than they used to be. They usually range from feeling awesome, dropping down to feeling good, but all in all, I am a happy chappie these days, thanks to meditation. It's all about the direction you're heading in and the journey you're travelling, not where you're currently at. If you're in a good place but moving away from it, it doesn't feel good. If you're in a bad place but moving towards a better place, it feels great. This is following your dharma. It's important to experience joy on your path, to bring happiness into every day, to be grateful and to treasure every moment. Don't sacrifice your daily bliss for big, long-term plans. This doesn't mean not having goals; it just means that if you are on the right road, following your dharma, inspired thought, and intuition, you should feel good and enjoy yourself. It should be exciting and fun. It's also about your "general" direction and not being too rigid. There will always be variations, fluctuations, and wrong turns. These lessons hold valuable wisdom within them. However, as long as you are using this knowledge to navigate and set a new course, making adjustments along the way, you're doing great.

"If you think about something, you will experience it. Whether it manifests into the material world or not, your thoughts are the same!" —MM

"EXERCISE"

WHY IS EXERCISE ON THE LIST?

Oh, did I mention that I am an Iron Man? Haha!
I even have an official Iron Man bob hat, cap, tattoo and socks now. I felt really good after completing this particular challenge and for what I had achieved. Not from an egotistical point of view or way of thinking, but from one of personal growth and triumph in the face of adversity. If I had listened to the programming I'd been given, I would be at least two surgeries in on each knee by now and never able to run again.

"When the song from within is louder than the music outside, you are manifesting."—MM

Exercise is on the list because I have learned that through endurance sport, you can achieve a "meditative state". Try saying this after two pints. It makes you "linger longer" in "Sharm-Hurghada". When I go running, swimming, or cycling, once I'm about one hour into my session, whatever I was thinking prior to that dissolves. It becomes low priority. It's like someone has a special mind comb and starts to remove all the knots in my head. Through exercise, you can end up in state of bliss. The bill you have to pay next week becomes low priority. Breathing becomes your main focus and putting one foot in front of the other is your number one task. Just like with Buddhist meditation, you end up inadvertently becoming fully present and focusing on the breath. Ask anyone who saw me doing Iron Man and they will tell you, I smiled from start to finish. I was fully present and in the moment the whole way round. My training didn't go according to plan, nothing like it was supposed to. Then the actual day itself was a catalogue of errors, just one mistake after another. Every bad decision a first-timer could make, I made it. However, I just remained calm, relaxed and didn't get frustrated or anxious. I didn't rush and just took "my time". After nearly sixteen hours I crossed the finish line and miraculously got round. Logic says I shouldn't have been able to manage it, but I did, with a big fat smile across my face. My mind was clear and I was in the now. All my problems disappeared and I was in bliss for sixteen hours, while everyone else was in agony. I was euphoric. They even wanted to interview three of us from Bolton Triathlon Club on the local radio station "Bolton FM", so we all went down to tell our tale. Next, Hollywood!

So it's a balance of exercise and meditation for me. These two are my essentials. I need the combination of both, for the best effects and results. One without the other and I definitely can feel my energy levels and joy diminish. I can feel a bit depleted and don't feel as good or cope as well. This duo, of nurturing the mind and the body, keeps me peaceful and healthy. It's a personal journey and so it's whatever works best for you. There are no rules.

Anyway, no more grunting and lifting weights for me. I have shed more than three stone and my entire big macho act! Well almost! Arggghhhhh! I get outside every opportunity I can now and I love it. I have been running around Entwistle reservoir at five in the morning with my head torch on, just as the sun is coming up. This is my favourite route because it is in nature and passes through some woodland. At this early hour, all the animals in the forest come out to say hello and good morning. I have seen deer, badgers, foxes, squirrels, and lots of different bird, to name but a few. It is just amazing. One of my favourite things is just me waking up with nature. This is very close to heaven on earth for the bald ex-builder!

IS MEDITATION THE ONLY WAY TO FIND INNER PEACE?

Absolutely. Yes. There is no other way. It's only meditation. Nothing else!

Just teasing again. No, it's whatever works for you. Meditation, however, is the only guaranteed method I know, that works for everyone who is willing. You might not become enlightened, but it will definitely reduce your stress levels and improve the quality of your life. Here is a list of just a few of the things that I do to find peace, that I do to become fully present in the moment and that can take me away to another realm. I have covered exercise already, as combined with meditation; it is an absolute must for me.

LONDON CONCERTANTE

This is a chamber orchestra, a mainly string ensemble, who tour up and down the country and now Europe, performing throughout the year. They usually choose incredible historic venues to perform in, which also have amazing acoustic properties, such as Manchester Cathedral, where I tend to go and watch them. They were on again at this venue whilst I was away in Egypt writing this book, so I had to miss the concert. I was gutted. I had four Class A tickets. This means that you get to sit in the first few rows.

I like to sit at the front because I love to watch them perform too, not just listen. It's fascinating to watch someone who gets completely lost in their passion, loving what they do. They connect with the instrument. It becomes an extension of their body and they become one. They express their emotions through the music, even within the confines of a set piece. I always take at least one person with me, usually more. It was the one thing that could have stopped me going to Egypt and I very nearly stayed at home, but I decided on this occasion that the book was more important.

"When you follow your dharma, there is no drama!"—MM

"EGYPT"

I knew that my dharma was to go and find solitude and write my story. I got really quiet and listened to the subtle energies and feelings in my body. My intuition is my direct line to God. It allows me to tune in and hear what the universe is trying to tell me. Forget logic; that's so yesterday. Follow your heart and your inner calling. You won't find your dharma by doing algebra, overthinking everything and worrying. Yes, before you say it, Alan Turing's dharma was probably to do algebra. You will find it by following your inspiration and doing what makes you feel good. Sometimes in order for me to do this, to make good choices and listen to my intuition, I need to go into the gap first and become still. I find most of my answers come to me in here, in the silence, or if not, just after I meditate, when my mind is quiet and clear.

Oh yes. So, to London Concertante. I have been to see them many times. Live classical music, predominantly strings with a harpsichord thrown in for good measure. Usually eight or nine members, performing together. For example, two violas, three violins, a bass, a harpsichord (which is a very old type of mini piano) and then, on some occasions, wait for it, an oboe. Hell yeah! An oboe is one of the hardest instruments to play, certainly that I have ever come across. It's all about breathing. While everyone else is casually taking a breath whenever they want, this guy has to get it perfect every time. He can only take a breath at certain key points during the performance, so as not to interrupt the flow. Sometimes these gaps are thirty to forty seconds apart and he is blowing the whole time. It's just absolutely amazing to watch. On one occasion, I needed a wee before the performance started, so I nipped off to the toilets. I stood at the urinal and had a quick chat with the guy next to me, about the weather. Twenty minutes later I saw him appear onstage. It was the same man I had been speaking to. It was the oboe guy. He hadn't got changed at that point, into his dinner suit and bow tie, ready for the show. I had no idea that he was a performer. We will never forget you, oboe guy.

So, London Concertante changed the way I saw the world and hence the course of my life.

Remember, "If you change the way you look at things, the things you look at change."—Dr Wayne Dyer

Time to get a tattoo, I think!

This was the first time I had experienced this incredible spectacle, and something wonderful had happened to me, because of my spiritual awakening or shift. I had never seen or heard anything so beautiful. I became very emotional. I then started to see beauty everywhere. A door that had been shut for a very long time had reopened and I had a connection into the spirit realm and with my true self once again. For the first time in years, I could see the light. This was the same week I went to Manjushri Buddhist Centre too. I was able to reconnect with my true feelings again and these emotions started to flood in on a regular basis after this. The orchestra do a rendition of *Oblivion* by Astor Piazzolla. This is an unusual Argentinean tango number. Wow. Each time I went back to watch them, I took more and more people with me. The last time I went, I took thirty people along. I wanted everyone to experience it, to see and feel the bliss and joy that I had. I have been six times now and, December 29th 2017 would have been my seventh. I had to give my tickets away in the end, but they went to a good home. I know at least one lady who feels like I do about them. Each time, the experience takes me away to another place and opens new doors. After my first visit I started to have very vivid memories from my childhood, remembering very specific smells and colours. Things that I had long since forgotten, buried deep in my mind, which I thought were gone for good. This was the start of something. I was rediscovering parts of myself and, in doing so, different forms of expression. From watching and listening to other people play music; I could understand what they were saying. I started to see beauty on a daily basis.

The next time this happened was in Edinburgh (I love Edinburgh, by the way). I went to a gallery to explore art and I got completely lost in it. Not in the gallery, silly! In the art. For the first time in my life I got it. It felt amazing. It was like I had put on a pair of special glasses that allowed me to see the emotions that were being conveyed in any particular piece.

So I had developed an appreciation for art too. I started to understand what people were trying to express through this medium. Then I looked at the time. I had been there for four hours and it felt like five minutes. You see, before I entered the gallery, I had decided to set no time constraints on this venture. I went "off the clock", having no allotted finish time. When you are fully present, time stops. You see, when you're in the perpetual "now", the external world clock keeps ticking, but time for you slows down or even stands completely still. You are in that one perfect moment continuously, rolling in ecstasy. There is a whole chapter on time in my next book and I go into this topic in much more detail. Ever wonder why a year seems inconceivable to a child, like an eternity, too long to comprehend? Yet to an older person the years fly by and time goes so quickly? Does time actually speed up and slow down or are children living in the moment, far more present and in the now than we are? All will be revealed!

NATURE

We should all take every available opportunity, daily if possible, to commune with nature. You see, when we immerse ourselves in a system where all living things operate within natural law, moving in harmony with each other, following their true nature and their dharma, we start to match that frequency. After all, we are also part of that system. Not man's system, but nature's system. We have just lost our way. If you are fully present in nature and go "off the clock", you start to reconnect with that system. I use this term when there are no time constraints on your activity. No rushing. No end time. Just free time. Time to be. This is when you start to see the magic in every landscape and in every living creature. You start to see with better eyes. This is when you really notice all the animals and that they seem to notice you too. It is "breath" taking. You see the common theme here? Whenever we become fully present, the breath becomes prevalent, again and again. Basically, whenever you are in the moment and at peace, it pops up. This perpetual subtle sensation arises once more, our attention and focus return to it. Breath is a very beautiful and constant reminder that we are still here, that we are alive, and that we should live every day experiencing bliss and joy. The breath won't always be there, but while it is, we need to experience life to its fullest potential. I know that the death of the body, the wrapping paper around the spirit and the true self, the shell that we see as humans in this lifetime, is not the end. We just leave it behind and simply go back home.

"We are all just walking each other home."—Ram Dass. Beautiful, isn't it?

We are always connected to the field and the flow of universal energy. So when a bird keeps coming to see you, or a squirrel looks straight at you, or a butterfly lands on your shoulder, this is God saying hello. We are all connected and communicate with each other through this field, this cosmic dance of energy. When loved ones have passed, they once again fully reconnect to this energy field, and nature is a great expression of this for them to utilise, to communicate with us. If you choose not to believe this, or if you're not fully present at that time, you will miss it. You have to be in the moment, and that means off the clock with your eyes wide open, to see the magic unfold. I know every time a robin comes to say hello to me, every time I see a deer is looking back at me through the trees, every time I see a cloud in the shape of a heart, that's my uncle Frank talking to me. Using the the unified field as his microphone and nature as his speaker! I have always had a special affinity with birds in nature. I think I was a bird in a past life and often dream of flying. On two occasions now they have flown into the front of my car on a busy motorway. I obviously slowed down and then pulled over to assess the situation, both to see if the bird was okay and also to view the damage to my car. In both instances, I avoided an accident up ahead, just moments later. Unfortunately, on both occasions, the birds died. I believe it was a warning and that they sacrificed their lives, to save mine. But it's up to you now. Only you can decide. It's whatever you choose to believe!

"If you want to change your world, change your mind."—MM
(Paraphrased from Norman Vincent Peale)

Even if it's 50/50 and you're just not sure, is it not worth exploring these things? Why not choose the 50% that leads to a path of bliss and a journey full of joy? Isn't this new world a better choice than living in fear, doubt, stress, and suffering? If you're bothered about what other people think, I don't want to labour the point, but stop it!
Have a word with yourself and pack it in!

"Peace is wherever you find it!"—MM

"THE SEA"

THE SEA AND GOING UNDERNEATH IT

I am not going to go into this too much here, because I think you get the idea now, it is whatever works for you, but this has to be on your bucket list. If you have ever done this you will know, it is like stepping off and entering into another world. The reason why scuba diving or even snorkelling can be so dangerous is because, until you get used to it, it is very easy to get completely lost in the activity. You can lose all track of time, depth, and any other aspect critical to breathing under water. You are swept away by the astounding beauty that lies beneath and get completely sucked into the moment. It's a must, and well worth the effort. It's the opposite of the next topic I will cover, skydiving. It is sublime and surreal; you are blinded by all the colours and the diversity of life. It's so amazing. It's epic, biblical even. In fact, it's really difficult not to be fully present when you're down there diving or snorkelling, ideally in a sunny climate and around a coral reef if possible. The sunlight penetrates the surface of the water and ignites all the colours below; it's like a fanfare of all God's creations on display. It's so incredible that you can't describe it properly, you can't do it justice, and you just have to experience it. Egypt, Sydney, the Cooke Islands; I snorkel whenever I am on my travels, every opportunity I get. I have done it in a quarry in Preston, but it's just not the same. It's not all that! If you've never done it, get your mask on, go and escape to another world, in this realm, right beneath your feet.

I love the analogy of a fish. When asked what his views are on water, he replies, "What's water?" You see, that's just like most of the human race in relation to spirit, the unified field, universal energy, God, or whatever you like to call it. It's all around us, it's in everything, it's in all of us, and it's what we are made of. We can't exist without it, it supports our very existence, and yet most of us can't or choose not to see it!

SKYDIVING AND ADRENALINE

This one's a bit of a cheat really. It's temporary and it's pleasure and I don't know about inner peace, but wow, I felt alive. By jumping out of an aeroplane I became fully present and in the moment, immersed in the realm of the five senses. When you're travelling at 110 mph straight down, you focus! You're certainly not worried about your gas bill when you're falling at terminal velocity from 12,000 feet.

"It's funny how fallin' feels like flyin', for a little while." — *Fallin' and Flyin'*, a song from the film *Crazy Heart*.

I included this quote for my friend Wesley. We sing this together.

You become very aware of your breath again and your heartbeat too! I did actually feel euphoria, joy, and then for several hours afterwards incredibly peaceful, in a state of bliss. I literally couldn't speak or hold a conversation until much later that evening; I was gobsmacked and lost for words. I couldn't stop smiling all day. I know this is not for everyone, but remember, it's just a ride. We never know when we are going to get off or when the ride is going to stop. Please don't let me go in my sleep. I want to be doing crazy stuff with whistles, balloons, and bells on, jumping naked off a bridge into a tin of beans maybe! Just teasing, I didn't mean it God. Sleep works just fine for me!

"To find the two, you must try the ten." —MM

If there are two things out there that are going to give you joy and happiness, you have to do new things to find them. Go on! Try something new. Make time for yourself. They might not all work for you, but you will never find the two that do if you don't try the ten. It's worth it! You're worth it! It's your life, your decision and your choice. It is up to you now, but please, go on, you owe it to yourself.

In an audiobook I listened to, Alan Watts said there is only one question, "To live or to die?" This doesn't mean mass suicide, it means addressing this dilemma whilst you're here, in this lifetime.

You have two choices, to follow your heart and your dharma living in joy, or to be a slave paralysed by fear. Please join me and start to play your music, sing your song.

You are amazing. You can do anything. Don't settle, don't make do, be the light that comes from within. It is your job to let it out.

You've tried the initial programming given to you. How did that work out?

Accept what is and let go of the past.

It's your time to shine!

Namaste Xx

ACKNOWLEDGEMENTS

A.H.Smith: My cousin, the artist and all-round amazing human being. He took the time to listen to my ideas and then turn my scribbles into the artwork that you see on the inside of this book. Thank you for donating your art to this book, Andrew.

Don Parry: A constant in my journey over the last twelve months. He is a friend, gifted poet, musician, and craftsman. He has shown me how to express myself by his example. What a beautiful man. Thank you for donating your poems to this book, Don.

Laurence Bell: A friend for many years and another Bolton author. Without his time, patience, and valuable advice this book would have taken so much longer.

Stephanie Currie: I can't imagine a world without you in it. You let me be me. You regularly feed me wonderful food and listen to me talk about my next book. It can't be easy for you, when I am brainstorming and discussing my latest off-the-wall ideas. You regularly hold council with me and also know how to fix me. You are a constant inspiration and shine brighter than any star. We are quantumly entangled. Q.E.

Carol McBride: My beautiful mum. She has supported me no matter what. I have been through some tough times and you were always there for me. For forty years I was a nightmare, but now that I am a divine being of light, your work is done. You can have a rest now. Just kidding Mum. Let's talk about it over a diet coffee. I know I am still difficult to manage. I love you and you are always in my thoughts.

Liam McBride – My brother and absolute hero. Without his help and support, this book simply wouldn't have been possible. Period.

To my family: We have been through a lot together, especially the last couple of years, but we are still here. United we stand. Thank you for all your ongoing support.

Earths Bounty, Bolton (Formerly "The Healthy Indulgence Cafe"): Just a quick note here. This was the first venue to give me a voice and to allow me to facilitate my meditation classes. I have been doing regular sessions here for over a year now, and will continue to do so. I have taught at many other beautiful venues too and met some genuinely incredible people, but this cafe has a special place in my heart. It is an eclectic community of spiritual people brought together by Dawn Woods and her family. They have one common goal, spreading peace and love. For its customers, it is a lighthouse of hope in a difficult world. It is far more than just an eatery and holistic centre. The whole is far greater than the sum of its parts. A very special place indeed.

Dr Wayne Dyer: A true legend. Over the past few years I have been heavily influenced by his work. His teachings have improved the quality of my life immeasurably and hence indirectly, that of all the people around me. I would also like to give a mention to Eckhart Tolle and Deepak Chopra at this point. They also played a very important part in my journey here, to happiness.

QUOTES

I have listed all the quotes from the book here. They are in order for your easy reference. A small number of the quotes have been used twice; this is intentional. The quotes in bold are associated with the pictures. MM refers to me, Midnight McBride. The majority of my quotes (MM) have been taken from the talks I have given over the last twelve months.

"When you think from a beautiful garden, you will see flowers everywhere!"—MM

"To be better than you were yesterday is a great achievement. Do this every single day. This is the path to enlightenment."—MM

"You can't build the truth on a lie."—MM

"You can start in the sewers and finish in the stars!"—MM

"You can go within, or go without."—MM (Paraphrased from Ralph Waldo Emerson)

"It takes great courage to step into the light."—MM

"The more light you emit, the more darkness is revealed!"—MM

"When you emit your inner light, you can see other people in the dark."—MM

"If you follow the herd, you won't be heard!"—MM

"Be the change that you wish to see in the world."—M. Gandhi

"You don't have to see the whole staircase. Just take the first step."—Martin Luther King Jr.

"All of humanity's problems stem from man's inability to sit quietly in a room alone."—Blaise Pascal

"Meditation is for everyone!"—MM

"To be told something once is to be informed. To be told something again and again is conditioning. You are now being programmed."—MM

"Rather a wild flower than a potted plant."—MM

"I am a human being, not a human doing."—Dr Wayne Dyer

"Once you label me, you negate me."—Dr Wayne Dyer

"Each time you raise yourself up, invite everyone to come and see the view."—MM

"It takes great courage to step into the light."—MM

"It's just a ride."—Bill Hicks

"The prisons we all live in are constructed by the mind."—MM

"The fools who dream."—*La La Land*

"The doors open inwards, and inside, there are no sides."—MM

"Once understood, freedom is an unstoppable force, because it is born of the mind."—MM

"The more you have, the less you see."—MM

"If every eight-year-old in the world is taught meditation, we will eliminate violence from the world within one generation."—Dalai Lama

"In order to fly, you must first learn how to spread your wings."—MM

"No matter what, someone always has to go first!"—MM

"If you want to sail far, you have to sail close to the wind."—MM

"If you don't jump, you can't fly."—MM

"The universe will correspond to the nature of your song."—Reverend Michael Beckwith

"If you change the way you look at things, the things you look at change."—Dr Wayne Dyer

"Make a life, not a living."—Dr Wayne Dyer

"If one advances confidently in the direction of his dreams, and endeavours to live the life that he has imagined, he will meet with a success unexpected in common hours."—Henry David Thoreau

"When you are inspired by some great purpose, some extraordinary project, all your thoughts break their bonds: Your mind transcends limitations, your consciousness expands in every direction, and you find yourself in a new, great and wonderful world. Dormant forces, faculties and talents become alive, and you discover yourself to be a greater person by far than you ever dreamed yourself to be."—Patanjali, *The Yoga Sutras of Patanjali*

"When you come to the end of the line, you have to go off the rails."—MM

"We are not human beings having a spiritual experience; we are spiritual beings having a human experience."—Dr Wayne Dyer

"The less you have, the more you see."—MM

"The more you have, the less you see."—MM

"We are all broken, that's how the light gets in."—Ernest Hemingway

"To appreciate sunlight, first you must stand in the shadows."—MM

"It's okay not to be okay. Once you are aware of this, your journey has begun!"—MM

"In order to learn anything, we have to talk about everything."—MM

"To err is human; to forgive, divine." Alexander Pope

"You can't fight water, but you can bathe in it."—MM

"As long as there are us and them, you can't have zen!"—MM

"More fighting never solved a war. Only peace can dissolve conflict."—MM

"War is complete madness. It is insanity personified. No exception!"—MM

"Those who are unaware they are walking in darkness will never seek the light."—Bruce Lee

"The harder the shell, the easier it cracks!"—MM

"An eye for an eye only ends up making the whole world blind."—M. Gandhi

"You can't build the truth on a lie."—MM

"Just like pouring gasoline onto a fire, more fighting never solved a war."—MM

"Fear a man who fears no consequence!"—MM

"The further down you start, the more remarkable your journey."—MM

"Thoroughly unprepared, we take the step into the afternoon of life. Worse still, we take this step with the false presupposition that our truths and our ideals will serve us as hitherto. But we cannot live the afternoon of life according to the program of life's morning, for what was great in the morning will be little at evening and what in the morning was true, at evening will have become a lie."—Carl Jung

"In order to learn anything, we have to talk about everything!" —MM

"In order to see what lies beneath, we need to get high!" —MM

"The higher you get, the more you can see." —MM

"Drink when you want to remember, don't drink when you want to forget, but remember, sobriety improves society." —MM

"If you want to bathe in the light, you must first know the dark." —MM

"When the sea is rough and the waves are high, you can't see land. But when the sea is calm and still, you can navigate with your vision." —MM

"When you are in the dark and you look around, you can see the light very clearly; do you have the courage to follow it? You have to move through the darkness to reach it. To transcend fear. That's where the answers lie. That's where you will find the truth. Everything you are seeking lies on the other side, waiting for you. It's always been there!" —MM

"Maktub!" —*The Alchemist* by Paulo Coelho

"When patterns are broken, new worlds emerge." —Tuli Kupferberg

"Through charity, comes clarity." —MM

"The music you hear inside is your dharma. Dance to it!"—MM

"If you want your life to flow, you have to let it all go."—MM

"If you keep saying "obl", you're going to have a wobble!"—MM

"If your motivations are born out of obligation, they are someone else's, not yours. You are following their wishes, not your dharma."—MM

"All anyone ever wants is peace, even if they don't know it yet."—MM

"Return of the Mack. Yes, it is..."—Mark Morrison

"Know thyself."—Socrates

"To thine own self be true."—Shakespeare

"If something is broken, in order to fix it, you must first take it apart and look inside."—MM

"To see celestial majesty, you have to retreat from the fire."—MM

"The closer to the light, the brighter you shine."—MM

"If you follow your own path, you can't get lost! When you're a pioneer, there is no map."—MM

"Unconditional love comes from unconditional thinking."—MM

"If you want a peaceful nation, practice meditation. It all starts with you."—MM

"Stress is mind created. Your stress is your problem!"—MM

"All problems, delusions and unhappiness are created by the mind. It is not our external circumstances or events that cause these feelings, but our thoughts about them and our reactions to them, that are responsible for our suffering. If we can learn to control our thoughts, we can be permanently happy and live in bliss. This can be achieved through a regular meditation practice."—MM

"In this universal intelligent system, everything is as it should be. Therefore, nothing is as it should be too. So there is nothing to worry about. It's all in divine order."—MM

"Thousands of candles can be lit from a single one, and its life will not be shortened. Happiness never decreases by being shared."—Buddha

"All power is from within and therefore under our control."—Robert Collier

"All that we are is the result of what we have thought."—Buddha

"Whether you think you can or think you can't, either way you are right."—Henry Ford

"The good news is that the moment you decide that what you know is more important than what you have been taught to believe, you will have shifted gears in your quest for abundance. Success comes from within, not from without." —Ralph Waldo Emerson

"Frustration is like shouting "Fire!" when you light a match; it makes a problem far bigger than it needs to be." —MM

"Regret is like tying a noose around the neck of the present moment and then pulling the rope tight. It strangles any chance of joy or bliss. Similarly, worry is like holding the present moment to ransom. Refusing to let it go until you get your desired outcome. This will never work; you will be forever a kidnapper, permanently holding the present moment captive. Never being able to enjoy your life. The universe doesn't respond to blackmail, it operates in complete harmony without resistance, it only responds to love." —MM

"The present moment has a round door; anything with sides can't get in." —MM

"No one ever dies from a snake bite; the venom that continues to pour through your system after the bite is what will destroy you." —Dr Wayne Dyer

"The wake can't drive the boat. It's just the trail that's left behind." —Alan Watts

"Your past doesn't define you. It is simply the view on the journey to this moment." —MM

"If you are always looking behind, you will trip up." —MM

"Whatever you focus on, you feed and move towards it." —MM

"Freedom is just another word for nothing left to lose!"—Janis Joplin

"In order to move forward, you have to let go of the ropes!"—MM

"Indecision is the thief of opportunity!"—Jim Rohn

"Don't fall down, fall forward. This is still progress!"—MM

"You miss 100% of the shots you don't take!"—Wayne Gretzky

"The prisons we all live in are constructed by the mind."—MM

"Be independent of the good opinion of other people."—Abraham Maslow

"You need to embrace the unknown until it becomes known."—MM

"You need to throw yourself into the realm of "infinite possibility" and practice "the wisdom of uncertainty.""—Deepak Chopra.

"Do less, accomplish more. This is the law of least effort."—Deepak Chopra

"You can go within, or go without."—MM (Paraphrased from Ralph Waldo Emerson)

"Infinite patience produces immediate results."—*A Course in Miracles*

"We need to disconnect from technology to reconnect with spirit."—MM

"Ten minutes in the bank, all day at the market."—Maharishi Mahesh Yogi

"Nobody has time. You have energy."—MM

"If you were on a train travelling overnight and you needed to sleep, would you find somewhere to rest? Yes! If you needed the toilet would you find a bathroom? Yes! Why can you not find a chair?"—Maharishi Mahesh Yogi.

"Have you got time to eat? Have you got time to breath? That's how important meditation is."—Geshe Kelsang Gyatso

"If you want to join the party, if you want to be party-pants, you have to be a participant."—MM

"Meditation is for everyone!"—MM

"To see celestial majesty, you have to retreat from the fire."—MM

"In the East they contemplate the forest; in the West we count the trees!"—Dr Wayne Dyer

"All of humanity's problems stem from man's inability to sit quietly in a room alone."—Blaise Pascal

"*No Jacket Required!*"—an album by Phil Collins

"Don't die with your music still in you!"—Dr Wayne Dyer

"If you let it, the universe can deliver at the speed of light!"—MM

"What you think of me is none of my business."—Dr Wayne Dyer

"This is easy, yes? This is how we meditate!"—Lewis Walch, my TM teacher

"The frequency you display attracts the people in your day!"—MM

"When your response to every situation is love, you have become the light."—MM

"You can't have world peace if everyone's not invited!"—MM

"In order to appreciate the light, you must first know the dark."—MM

"This too shall pass!"—Ancient proverb

"Frustration is like shouting "Fire!" when you light a match; it makes a problem far bigger than it needs to be."—MM

"The ancestor to every action is a thought!"—Ralph Waldo Emerson

"Imagination is everything. It is the preview of life's coming attractions!"—Albert Einstein

"Be mindful of your thoughts, young Padawan!"—*Star Wars: Episode 1 – The Phantom Menace*

"If you follow your own path, you can't get lost! When you're a pioneer, there is no map."—MM

"If we all Om together, we will have peace forever."—MM

"What you oppose never goes!"—MM

"Whatever you focus on, you feed and move towards it."—MM

"You're the MD of your thoughts and the CEO of your inner peace. It's your business!"—MM

"Ten minutes in the bank, all day at the market."—Maharishi Mahesh Yogi

"Your miracles are an inside job."—Dr Wayne Dyer

"When you do good, you feel good!"—MM

"Not Buddha yet!"—*Chicken Soup for the Soul*

"What you think of me is none of my business."—Dr Wayne Dyer

"To err is human; to forgive, divine."—Alexander Pope

"We are not human beings having a spiritual experience; we are spiritual beings having a human experience."—Dr Wayne Dyer

"Forgiveness is the fragrance that the violet sheds on the heel that has crushed it."—Mark Twain

"Before every major success come many minor failures."—MM

"In order to be the most improved, you have to start at the bottom. To be truly remarkable, you must first be truly terrible. This is growth. This is progress. This is evolution!"—MM

"If I could go back, would I do things differently? Yes, of course. I have evolved and grown. So do you regret anything? No, of course not. That's how I have evolved and grown."—MM

"If you don't make changes, you will never see change."—MM

"Let go and let God."—Dr Wayne Dyer

"We are all broken. That's how the light gets in."—Ernest Hemingway

"You have to keep breaking your heart until it opens."—Rumi

"The wound is the place where the light enters you."—Rumi

"Through adversity and trauma comes peace. We can then open new doors and experience the divine."—MM

"A man who thinks he knows everything knows very little. A man who realises how little he knows may know something!"—MM

"In Lak'ech."—Mayan greeting

"The universe will correspond to the nature of your song."—Reverend Dr Michael Beckwith

"Everything's going to be alright!"—*No Woman No Cry* by Bob Marley

"If you knew who walks beside you on this path that you have chosen, fear would be impossible." —*A Course in Miracles*

"If you think about something, you will experience it. Whether it manifests into the material world or not, your thoughts are the same!"—MM

"When the song from within is louder than the music outside, you are manifesting."—MM

"When you follow your dharma, there is no drama!"—MM

"If you change the way you look at things, the things you look at change."—Dr Wayne Dyer

"We are all just walking each other home."—Ram Dass. Beautiful, isn't it?

"If you want to change your world, change your mind."—MM (Paraphrased from Norman Vincent Peale)

"Peace is wherever you find it!"—MM

"It's funny how fallin' feels like flyin', for a little while."— *Fallin' and Flyin'* from *Crazy Heart*

"To find the two, you must try the ten."—MM

"Mind first, bum second!"—MM

BIBLIOGRAPHY

All the statistics I have referenced in the book are listed here. Most of them have simply been researched on the internet using Google and Wikipedia:

The Matrix, directed by Andy Wachowski and Larry Wachowski. 1999; Burbank, CA: Warner Bros. Pictures.

Brodie, Richard. *Virus of the Mind: The New Science of the Meme.* Carlsbad, CA: Hay House, Inc., 2009.

Spotlight, directed by Tom McCarthy. 2015; Los Angeles, CA: Open Road Films.

The Men Who Made Us Spend (episode 2), directed by Claire Burnett. 2014; London: BBC.

Poltergeist, directed by Tobe Hooper. 1982; Beverly Hills, CA: Metro-Goldwyn-Mayer Studios Inc.

The Waltons (season 7, episode 5, *The Changeling*), directed by Lawrence Dobkin. 1978; New York City, NY: CBS.

Star Wars: Episode I – The Phantom Menace, directed by George Lucas. 1999; Los Angeles, CA: 20th Century Fox.

To date, over $85 million has been paid out to 552 victims.
Source:https://www.washingtonpost.com/news/acts-of-faith/wp/2017/07/29/he-was-a-priest-central-to-the-spotlight-child-sex-abuse-scandal-now-hes-a-free-man/?noredirect=on&utm_term=.0b99c8aa09d8

Two other things that I now know can recreate this balance are certain pieces of classical music and meditation. This has been scientifically proven.
Source:https://www.limelightmagazine.com.au/news/study-shows-that-music-can-rewire-the-brain/
Source:https://eocinstitute.org/meditation/research-on-meditation-how-modern-science-is-proving-the-benefits-of-meditation/

The Iraq War death toll:
British soldier deaths   179
American solider deaths   4,488
Iraqi deaths   500,000 +
Source: http://www.bbc.co.uk/news/uk-10637526
Source:http://www.nydailynews.com/news/national/new-study-shows-shocking-cost-iraq-war-article-1.1290568

Various sources report wildly different figures about civilian casualties, but the lowest is 165,000 and the highest is at 600,000.
Source:https://en.wikipedia.org/wiki/Casualties_of_the_Iraq_War

The US Navy's Nimitz class aircraft carriers, for example, weighing in at more than 100,000 tons of metal. They are up to 330 metres long, can house a crew of up to 5,000, and carry more than 70 fighter jets. A floating bringer of death that takes years to build and is specifically designed to kill humans en masse, with large guns, rockets, and bombs. Oh, and the cost is about $9 billion dollars per unit.
Source:https://en.wikipedia.org/wiki/Nimitz-class_aircraft_carrier

250,000 boys between the ages of 14 and 18 served in the British Army during World War One. The youngest was found to be just 12. The average life expectancy in the trenches was just six weeks. They were sent off to almost certain death.
Source: http://www.bbc.co.uk/guides/zcvdhyc
Source: https://www.warhistoryonline.com/articles/40-plus-1-fascinating-facts-about-wwi.html

Do you know that more US troops committed suicide after they returned home from Iraq and Afghanistan than were actually killed in combat?
Source:https://www.mercurynews.com/2015/11/10/veterans-day-suicide-has-caused-more-american-casualties-than-wars-in-iraq-and-afghanistan/

Did you know that at least 30% of all these troops develop mental health problems within three months of arriving home?
Source:https://en.wikipedia.org/wiki/Casualties_of_the_Iraq_War

There is a reason why the highest killer of men under the age of forty in this country is suicide.
Source:https://www.esquire.com/uk/culture/a9202/britain-male-suicide-crisis/
Source:https://www.theguardian.com/society/2015/feb/19/number-of-suicides-uk-increases-2013-male-rate-highest-2001

The US has hit three hospitals in recent years, for example. Directly in Iraq and Afghanistan, and then a third by US-backed rebel groups in Syria.
Source:https://www.commondreams.org/news/2016/12/09/us-military-admits-we-deliberately-bombed-hospital-iraq
Source:https://edition.cnn.com/2016/04/29/politics/u-s-airstrike-hospital-afghanistan-investigation/index.html
Source:https://www.theguardian.com/world/2016/jul/20/us-airstrike-allegedly-kills-56-civilians-in-northern-syria

Dr David Kelly spoke out about our plans to invade Iraq under false pretences, which was highly inconvenient, and he was then found dead two days later. He had been nominated for a Nobel Peace Prize. He was a top weapons expert and yet apparently took his own life with "a blunt garden knife". Lord Hutton tried to suppress the release of the post mortem for seventy years with a secrecy order, to "protect the family".
Source: http://www.bbc.co.uk/news/uk-13716127

One in four people in the UK will experience a mental health problem "each year".
Source: McManus, Sally, et al. (2009). "Adult Psychiatric Morbidity in England, 2007: Results of a Household Survey". The NHS Information Centre for Health and Social Care.

One in six people report experiencing a common mental health problem (such as anxiety and depression) in any given week.
Source: McManus, Sally, et al. (eds.) (2016). "Mental Health and Wellbeing in England: Adult Psychiatric Morbidity Survey 2014". Leeds: NHS Digital.

According to Occupational Health and Safety news and the National Council on Compensation of Insurance, up to 90% of all visits to primary care physicians are for stress-related complaints.
Source: Salleh, Mohd. Razali. "Life Event, Stress and Illness." *The Malaysian Journal of Medical Sciences* 15, no. 4 (2008): 9–18. Print.

"Kadampa Buddhism is a Mahayana Buddhist school founded by the great Indian Buddhist Master Atisha (AD 982-1054).
In the word, 'Kadampa', 'Ka' refers to Buddha's teachings, and 'dam' to Atisha's special Lamrim instructions. Kadampas, then, are practitioners who regard Buddha's teachings as personal instructions and put them into practice by following the instructions of Lamrim.
By integrating their understanding of all Buddha's teachings into their practice of Lamrim, and by integrating their experience of Lamrim into their everyday lives, Kadampas use Buddha's teachings as practical methods for transforming daily activities into the path to enlightenment."
Source: www.kadampa.org

So visualisation techniques, not just within a meditation, have been proven to work scientifically. They are such powerful techniques that they are used by NASA and the US Olympic team.
Source:https://www.nasa.gov/centers/ames/research/technology-onepagers/intel_virtual_station.html
Source:https://www.washingtonpost.com/sports/olympics/for-olympians-seeing-in-their-minds-is-believing-it-can-happen/2016/07/28/6966709c-532e-11e6-bbf5-957ad17b4385_story.html?utm_term=.8ef277bbe657

Did you know that the average child laughs more than three hundred times a day? And wait for it, the average adult just fifteen.
Source:http://www.aath.org/do-children-laugh-much-more-often-than-adults-do

It is said that twenty minutes doing TM can be the equivalent to having several hours of sleep.
Source: https://www.tm.org/
Source:https://www.artofliving.org/meditation/meditation-for-you/meditation-sleep

ABOUT THE AUTHOR—

MIDNIGHT MCBRIDE

Hello, everyone. I hope you all got something positive from my book. I am a meditation teacher and guest speaker working predominantly around the Northwest of England.

I have two goals:

To teach as many people as possible to meditate, to enable them to reduce stress, think correctly, and find inner peace. Also, to show that we all make mistakes and that is part of the learning process. Hopefully, by my example, people can see that if I can do it then anyone can.

The difference between someone in a state of bliss and someone stood next to them in severe distress is simply the way they are thinking. Your thoughts create your reality. Correct thought through meditation is more important than food. Your body can go several days without food. If your mind is unhealthy, you could have a serious accident or, even worse, take your own life. You may not make it through the day. In our society, we tend to put the mind way down on the list of our priorities, putting our bodies and social lives first. Although these are both important aspects, they should be secondary to the mind. I aim to show people that correct thought and good mental health should be right at the very top.

"Mind first, bum second!" —MM

This book has been a difficult and yet wonderful journey for me. I have now found a medium that has enabled me to express myself. I have already written a second book in note form and I am now on my third. I hope that with your help and support, I can continue to do so.

Whilst this book is being launched, I will be setting up a YouTube channel, releasing some of the videos from my workshops and talks over the last twelve months. However, it is unlikely to be ready in time for the sale of this book. It should be in place soon after though. I also have various social media channels, all listed below. I have a new website too, but it is very basic at the moment while the main one is being built.

FACEBOOK

https://www.facebook.com/MidnightMcBrideOfficial/

INSTAGRAM

https://www.instagram.com/midnight_mcbride/

TWITTER -

https://twitter.com/MidnightMcBride

www.wise-up.co.uk

Supported by Liam and Mark at

Wise-Up Addiction Awareness Ltd

Reg Nr: 10915378

Email: info@wise-up.co.uk

Web: ww.wise-up.co.uk

WEBSITE

http://www.midnightmcbride.com

EMAIL

midnightmcbride@gmail.com

Once it is ready, you will be able to find my YouTube channel by searching for –

Midnight McBride